Basic Bible TEACHINGS

An Introduction to the Lutheran Faith

CONCORDIA PUBLISHING HOUSE · SAINT LOUIS

Participant Book

3558 S. Jefferson Ave., St. Louis, MO 63118-3968
1-800-325-3040 • www.cph.org

Edited by Lisa Clark, Barbara Szofran, and Brenda Trunkhill

Thank you to the pastors who helped us better understand the needs of those new to the Lutheran Christian faith.

Manufactured in the United States of America

7 8 9 10 11 26 25

CONTENTS

1. Living with Expectations 4
   God Gives Us Value 6
   God Gives Us Grace 7
   God Gives Us Expectations 8
   God Gives Us the Law 12
   God Gives Us the Gospel 13
   God Gives Us Strength 14

2. Living with Jesus as Savior 18
   God Gives Us His Word 19
   God Gives Us Law and Gospel 20
   God Gives Us Salvation's Story 21
   God Gives Us Faith 23
   God Gives Us Righteousness 25

3. Living as God's Child 30
   God Gives Us New Life 31
   God Gives Us a Name 33
   God Gives Us What We Need 34
   God Gives Us Peace 36
   God Gives Us Free Will 37
   God Gives Us Prayer 38

4. Living the Christian Life 44
   God Gives Us Purpose 45
   God Gives Us Freedom 46
   God Gives Us Forgiveness 49
   God Gives Us the Church 52
   God Gives Us Worship 54
   God Gives Us a Commission 56

5. Living Forever with Jesus 60
   God Gives Us Eternal Life 61

6. Appendix 63
   * Glossary 63
   * Historical Background 67
   * Lutheran Liturgy 70
   * Church Year Calendar 72

Six Chief Parts (Quick Reference)
   * The Ten Commandments 10
   * The Apostles' Creed 24
   * Holy Baptism 32
   * The Lord's Prayer 40
   * Confession 48
   * Holy Communion 50

CHAPTER 1

Living with Expectations

Basic Bible Teachings

High Achievement

Our culture puts a lot of emphasis on top performance and achievement. We try to prove ourselves to others and show we're valuable, even vital, to the team. We try to make ourselves stand out compared to others. We want to succeed and to be the best, and we want others to notice when we do!

Independence

© iStock / Yuri Arcus

We're expected to be in control of the situation—all situations. We've got to keep it together—always. Sometimes, it seems that there's no room for mistakes and that we fail when we need help from others. It's easier just to pretend everything's fine than to admit that things aren't perfect.

Community

But at the same time, we're expected to be a part of the group. There's a constant pressure to stay connected, to be accountable, to be a team player. Communication is a huge priority in our culture, and we need to be ready to respond to any request. In this setting where media is social and interactive, we're also expected to get along with everyone, even to the point of keeping quiet if our opinions might cause tension.

What does God expect of us?

Our God is a **holy** God, and He requires that same holiness from His people. **Jesus** says, "You therefore must be perfect, as your heavenly Father is perfect" (Matthew 5:48). God's expectations are different from those of the world, and they're nothing short of perfect holiness.

BUT . . .

Because of **sin**, we will never measure up to God's perfection. It doesn't take a long look at ourselves to realize we are far from being the perfect employee, friend, student, spouse, father, or mother. Because of sin, we can't accomplish everything on our own. It seems like things rarely go according to plan.

Because of sin, we deserve only punishment for those thoughts that are selfish, for those words that lie and hurt others, and for those actions that are immoral or impure.

BUT . . .

What does God tell us in His Holy Word?

"For our sake He made [Jesus] to be sin who knew no sin, so that in [Jesus] we might become the righteousness of God" (2 Corinthians 5:21).

Because of Jesus, our achievement is found in what He accomplished for us—**forgiveness** and life with Him.

Because of Jesus, our weakness and dependence are placed on Him who gives us strength.

Because of Jesus, we are given more than a community. We are part of a family, taking joy in serving others.

"For **GOD**
so loved the world,
that He gave His only **Son**,
that whoever believes
in Him should not
perish but have
eternal life."
(John 3:16)

God Gives Us Value

How do we judge the value of something? We look at it, analyze it, assess it, and then we determine: *Is it worth anything to us?* We expect God to act like us, to analyze our value and determine if we are worth anything to Him. That's how our **sinful nature** thinks. We *want* to think that God judges us according to how we perform. It would make this whole **salvation** thing a *lot* easier to understand. In fact, most religions do teach that people have to earn their way to **heaven** (or some sort of spiritual higher level). Other religions will ask you to always be evaluating yourself with these kinds of questions:

- How many good deeds have you done today?
- Did you find your inner peace?
- Did you make a decision to follow God?

Other religions will ask you to be bold and strong and self-reliant with statements such as these:

- It's up to you to be good.
- It's up to you to attain control of your mind.
- It's up to you to turn your life around.

You. You. You. That's how most religions work, but **Lutheran** Christianity is different. Lutherans teach that our value is not based on what we do or don't do. Our worth is not determined by what we can contribute or earn. It isn't even based on who we are on the inside. Our value is based on who God is, what God does, and who He says we are because of Jesus **Christ**!

God is almighty, and He uniquely designed the world—all that is in it—especially each one of us. We are His creatures; in God's eyes, that gives us value.

We messed up the whole perfect **creation** thing with sin, but God is **merciful**. He immediately promised our first parents after they brought sin into the world that He would fix it. God would send a **Savior**, a conqueror of sin and **death**, and that Savior would be Himself. A God who dies *for* His people—that should tell us a lot about our value in God's eyes.

In *Basic Bible Teachings*, we will learn about the great lengths God goes to on our behalf because we are His valued children. That's the story of the entire **Bible**: God's plan of salvation. It is through this story of who our Savior Jesus is and what He did for us that we will truly learn the extent of God's love and what that means in our lives.

What's Your Score?

How do you rate yourself? God demands a perfect ten, all the time, in all areas of your life. "For whoever keeps the whole law but fails in one point has become accountable for all of it" (James 2:10). We can never perform well enough to attain the perfection that our holy God expects and demands. "For all have sinned and fall short of the glory of God" (Romans 3:23).

But our Savior took our place and lived a perfect life for us. He died for us so that we may have life. "For the wages of sin is death, but the free gift of God is eternal life in Christ Jesus our Lord" (Romans 6:23). It is only because of Jesus that we are able to have a relationship with God and value in His eyes.

God Gives Us Grace

God doesn't keep score the way the world does. God doesn't accept people based on intelligence, performance, intentions, attitudes, or any other humanly measurable trait. Why? Because of sin, we cannot ever be perfect and holy enough to be in the presence of God. He is holy; we are not!

Read the story of the workers in the vineyard from Matthew 20:1–16. The **kingdom** of heaven is not for those who work the hardest, understand the most, or put in the most effort to live the best lives. The kingdom of heaven, the vineyard, is for those whom Jesus *calls* to be in His vineyard. In this **parable**, the workers who are called early are eventually sent out of the vineyard because they resented the **mercy** of the Master. Those who were called later remained in the vineyard, trusting the Master, dependent on His mercy and care for them.

BUT THIS DOESN'T MAKE SENSE!

Many people just don't understand this—those in Jesus' time and those in our own time.

The parables aren't the only place where Jesus humbled the proud and lifted up the humble. Jesus ate with sinners, walked with sinners, healed sinners, talked with sinners, called sinners to be **disciples**. Jesus interacted with social groups typically ignored or shunned—He welcomed little children, conversed

with cultural outcasts, talked to sinful adulterers. And, completely flipping convention on its head, Jesus spoke *against* the teachers of the law, who were supposed to be the godly people, the high achievers. It just didn't make sense.

God desires us to have a humble and contrite heart. He expects us to listen to what He tells us in His **Word**. There, He tells us we are sinners. There, He tells us we can never work our way to perfection.

God then tells us in His Word that even though we are sinners, He sent us a Savior to pay the penalty of our sins, to make us holy, to give us perfection we didn't earn. How can we believe this? It just doesn't make sense.

The Bible tells us that God is love and shows us how He acts according to that love. Through the **Holy Spirit** working through His Word, He gives us **faith**.

God gives us the ability to believe what makes no sense at all. Then, through faith, we believe it when God says how weak and dependent we are—how utterly *not* in control we are. Through faith, we hear and believe that Christ is our merciful Master who calls us into His kingdom, cares for us, strengthens us, and makes us a part of His family forever.

All this love is a special, undeserved love called **grace**. Because we're sinners, we don't deserve the **blessings** that God gives us; because we're sinners, we could never earn His favor. Because of Christ, He gives this all to us anyway—because He loves us, because He wants to be with us forever. How, again, do we get this grace, this faith? God tells us in the Bible that it is received, not earned:

"For by grace you have been saved through faith. And this is not your own doing; it is the gift of God, not a result of works, so that no one may boast"

(Ephesians 2:8-9).

Living with Expectations

God Gives Us Expectations

Do you see why this grace means so much to us? If we didn't believe we were sinners who needed a Savior from sin, we wouldn't appreciate the magnitude of what God has done for us. Lutherans call this **Law** (seeing our sin) and **Gospel** (seeing our Savior).

God tells us exactly what He expects from us through the Ten Commandments. Jesus summarizes the Law like this: **"You shall love the Lord your God with all your heart and with all your soul and with all your mind and with all your strength" (Mark 12:30).**

That is the most important commandment because every other commandment is dependent on your ability to keep that one. In fact, the first three commandments all describe how to show love to God.

Jesus gives this as the second most important commandment:

"You shall love your neighbor as yourself" (Mark 12:31).

© iStock / Eva Katalin Kondoros

And that really means putting others *first*. The Fourth through the Tenth Commandments describe how we show love to others. So why is it so hard to put others first? Because of our sin (inside and out), our first reaction is to get defensive and to look out for our own interests. We need money, a home, nice clothes, fun times, great cars. Even our society pushes the idea that we need to achieve our own dreams at all cost and keep anyone from getting in our way.

We don't want to inconvenience ourselves or make a sacrifice to help others if it means giving up some of our own time or things. In all we do, we live for the day—for what's enjoyable at the moment—not thinking about how our words and actions may affect others.

Dig a Little Deeper

READ Jonah 3:1–4:2 to see how God showed grace to the Ninevites.

READ Luke 15:11–32 to see how God is like the forgiving father who showed grace to his son.

Missing the Mark

Professional baseball players spend huge amounts of their days and nights practicing and playing the game, so you'd think they'd be perfect, right? Hardly!

Do batters hit a home run each time they step up to the plate? To earn a .300 batting average, which is considered good, a player hits the ball and gets on base only three times out of ten. And most likely, those hits are not even home runs.

Do pitchers throw a strike whenever they want to? Surely they *wish* they'd never walk anyone!

When we sin, we miss the target—we don't do what we should. We fail to live up to God's perfect expectations. Sure, we'll keep some commandments; even with a failing "record," we may fool others into thinking we're good people. But deep inside, we're all sinful. Sin is every thought, desire, word, and deed that goes against God's Law.

If God kept a record of all of our sins, no one could stand before our holy God. But the Gospel is that with Him, there is hope and forgiveness.

"Hope in the Lord! For with the Lord there is steadfast love, and with Him is plentiful redemption."

(Psalm 130:7)

Picture Perfect

How do you picture what the perfect spouse (or another family member) would act like? Always cheerfully doing the household chores? giving you plenty of affection? showing you how important you are? communicating clearly so there's no misunderstanding? putting your own interests first?

How do you picture the perfect employee or student? Always cheerfully getting work done on time or early? doing every job perfectly? being a pleasant person to work with on projects? complimenting others? going above and beyond what's expected? looking for ways to encourage others and to help them to succeed?

"A new commandment I give to you, that you love one another: just as I have loved you, you also are to love one another." (John 13:34)

Our selfish nature continually makes us concentrate most on what makes *us* happy. By spending all that time on doing things that we enjoy and that give us pleasure, you'd think we'd be happy people! But looking at our lives, we see that things are nowhere near picture perfect.

So why would God give us all these commandments focused solely on how to treat *others*? Try to imagine a world where everyone obeyed these commandments. There would be no stealing, no murder, no sexual sins, no angry or jealous thoughts or plotting, no envy of other people. *That* would be true joy! But we all fail to keep these commandments, daily—every one of us. Should we be surprised that the world seems like such a mess? Should we be surprised that we're not all happy people? Happiness is an emotion that comes and goes, based on circumstances; true joy is lasting and stronger, based on God-given peace and contentment. We feel joy when we serve others, not when we think first of our own desires.

The Ten Commandments

From Luther's Small Catechism

Basic Bible Teachings

The First Table of the Law: Our Relationship with God

I

The First Commandment

You shall have no other gods.

What does this mean? We should fear, love, and trust in God above all things.

II

The Second Commandment

You shall not misuse the name of the LORD your God.

What does this mean? We should fear and love God so that we do not curse, swear, use satanic arts, lie, or deceive by His name, but call upon it in every trouble, pray, praise, and give thanks.

III

The Third Commandment

Remember the Sabbath day by keeping it holy.

What does this mean? We should fear and love God so that we do not despise preaching and His Word, but hold it sacred and gladly hear and learn it.

Keeping God's Commandments

God told His people, "If you faithfully obey the voice of the LORD your God, being careful to do all His commandments that I command you today, the LORD your God will set you high above all the nations of the earth. And all these blessings shall come upon you and overtake you, if you obey the voice of the LORD your God" (Deuteronomy 28:1–2). The promise of blessing if *all* of His Commandments are kept? Life will be good!

But if *all* of the Commandments aren't kept: "If you will not obey the voice of the LORD your God or be careful to do all His commandments and His statutes that I command you today, then all these curses shall come upon you and overtake you" (Deuteronomy 28:15). We're doomed! We can't keep all of these Commandments! They **condemn** us as sinners who need God's mercy.

Thankfully, that isn't the end of the story. "Christ redeemed us from the curse of the law by becoming a curse for us—for it is written, 'Cursed is everyone who is hanged on a tree'—so that in Christ Jesus . . . we might receive the promised Spirit through faith" (Galatians 3:13–14). Jesus took the curse upon Himself! We are no longer doomed! **Praise** be to God! But God's Commandments are still to be followed so that our lives will be the way God intended: loving and trusting Him above all and loving our neighbors as ourselves. That's what God knows is best for us.

The Second Table of the Law: Our Relationship with Others

IV

The Fourth Commandment

Honor your father and your mother.

What does this mean? We should fear and love God so that we do not despise or anger our parents and other authorities, but honor them, serve and obey them, love and cherish them.

V

The Fifth Commandment

You shall not murder.

What does this mean? We should fear and love God so that we do not hurt or harm our neighbor in his body, but help and support him in every physical need.

VI

The Sixth Commandment

You shall not commit adultery.

What does this mean? We should fear and love God so that we lead a sexually pure and decent life in what we say and do, and husband and wife love and honor each other.

VII

The Seventh Commandment

You shall not steal.

What does this mean? We should fear and love God so that we do not take our neighbor's money or possessions, or get them in any dishonest way, but help him to improve and protect his possessions and income.

VIII

The Eighth Commandment

You shall not give false testimony against your neighbor.

What does this mean? We should fear and love God so that we do not tell lies about our neighbor, betray him, slander him, or hurt his reputation, but defend him, speak well of him, and explain everything in the kindest way.

IX

The Ninth Commandment

You shall not covet your neighbor's house.

What does this mean? We should fear and love God so that we do not scheme to get our neighbor's inheritance or house, or get it in a way which only appears right, but help and be of service to him in keeping it.

X

The Tenth Commandment

You shall not covet your neighbor's wife, or his manservant or maidservant, his ox or donkey, or anything that belongs to your neighbor.

What does this mean? We should fear and love God so that we do not entice or force away our neighbor's wife, workers, or animals, or turn them against him, but urge them to stay and do their duty.

The Close of the Commandments

What does God say about all these commandments?

He says, "I, the Lord your God, am a jealous God, punishing the children for the sin of the fathers to the third and fourth generation of those who hate Me, but showing love to a thousand generations of those who love Me and keep My commandments." (Ex. 20:5–6)

What does this mean? God threatens to punish all who break these commandments. Therefore, we should fear His wrath and not do anything against them. But He promises grace and every blessing to all who keep these commandments. Therefore, we should also love and trust in Him and gladly do what He commands.

God Gives Us the Law

God has expectations for us. One way of talking about His expectations is by talking about His Law. One way to look at the Law is to see that **it keeps us from doing wrong.** If you're afraid of being punished or getting in trouble, you're more likely to follow the law. A *curb* keeps cars where they belong—on the street. The Law restrains us so that we are kept within safe boundaries.

The Law also shows us our sin. When we look in a *mirror* (especially a magnified mirror!), we see how we truly look, blemishes and all. When we take a close look at our thoughts—the state of our heart—and actions (or lack of actions), we are convicted. We know we've done wrong.

Another way the Law is used is as a *guide*. **The Law shows us how to live.** We can see from the Law what God expects of us as His children. "By this all people will know that you are My disciples, if you have love for one another" (John 13:35). We know that we cannot live up to this perfectly. We realize we need help and forgiveness. This makes us ready to hear the Gospel, the source of help and forgiveness.

Facing Our Sins

Some say Christianity is a religion based on fear, that we pretend to be holy because we fear God's **judgment**. But after a quick look around, we all can see and experience that God's judgment against sin has already happened: sickness, disease, violence, natural disasters, and especially death. These are the effects of sin we see each day. It's a reality that our world and all the people in it are no longer perfect. This has been true since **the fall** into sin.

Christianity is not a religion of fear; it is a religion of hope. The temporal effects of sin remain in this life, but the **eternal** penalty of sin has been removed through Christ.

What happens if you fail to hit the target of perfect behavior? A penalty must be paid! Our holy God demands holy behavior. When you sin, you deserve God's righteous wrath and punishment.

When Adam and Eve sinned, they brought the promised consequence of sin into the world—death (Romans 6:23). What is death? There are two kinds: physical and eternal. We know physical death; we see it all around us. Eternal death is the total and forever separation from God. Because of sin, it is the state in which you are conceived and born.

Just as children today inherit qualities from their parents, so we, all humankind, inherit **original sin** from our original parents. Our desire to sin (sinful nature) has been passed along from generation to generation. "I was brought forth in iniquity, and in sin did my mother conceive me" (Psalm 51:5). Original sin

- brings **guilt** and condemnation to all people;
- leaves us without a true fear and love of God;
- makes us spiritually blind, dead, and enemies of God; and
- causes us to commit all our daily sins in thought, desires, words, and deeds.

Here is a simple summary: We don't have a sinful nature because we sin. We sin because we have a sinful nature.

Is Satan real? Many don't think so, but **Satan** is a real, living being. He is the originator of all wickedness (Ephesians 2:2). He was an **angel** of God, but he rebelled against Him. Now he prowls the earth, seeking to destroy the children of God. Another name for Satan is the **devil**, which means "accuser" (Revelation 12:10); he uses lies to accuse and "build a case against" God's people and even God's Word. Satan tempts and entraps God's people into guilt and sin. Because of our sinful nature, Satan's **temptations** are overbearing. He has minions, countless fallen angels, working for him to attack God's people and destroy their faith.

God Gives Us the Gospel

Our hope and defense against Satan is the Gospel—that Jesus has bound the devil and rescued us from his dominion. Jesus has won the victory (1 Corinthians 15:57). Only in Jesus and His teaching will anyone be free from sin, death, and the devil's rule. "If you abide in My word, you are truly My disciples, and you will know the truth, and the truth will set you free. . . . If the Son sets you free, you will be free indeed" (John 8:32, 34, 36). Each day, we're bombarded with information online, in the media, and even from family and friends. How can we know who is telling the truth?

There is peace knowing that God's Word is truth. We can filter everything we hear through the **Scriptures**. Jesus said, **"I am the way, and the truth, and the life. No one comes to the Father except through Me" (John 14:6)**. Through faith—believing in Jesus as our Savior—Jesus has set us free. We are free from worry, from regret, from fear that we aren't good enough, rich enough, special enough. Through faith, we have hope not only for eternal life that God has promised, but also that the struggles and challenges we face today are in God's hands. Faith trusts God even when we don't understand.

"Faith is the assurance of things hoped for, the conviction of things not seen." (Hebrews 11:1)

We may not understand God's purposes, but we can trust His promises are true: "Not one word has failed of all the good things that the Lord your God promised concerning you. All have come to pass for you; not one of them has failed" (Joshua 23:14). There is freedom in trusting that Jesus is the truth.

© iStock / Pattie Calfy

The Truth Will Set You Free

The true feeling of having a weight off your shoulder is being free of the power of sin. It's trusting that everything is right between you and God because of Christ. True peace is not being stress-free in this life or not having to experience pain and suffering. True peace is trusting in God—knowing that your sins are forgiven and that you have an all-powerful God taking care of you now and for all eternity.

This peace helps us endure anything we go through in this life because we know we can trust our loving God to be with us through it all. "Therefore, since we have been justified by faith, we have peace with God through our Lord Jesus Christ. . . . Not only that, but we rejoice in our sufferings, knowing that suffering produces endurance, and endurance produces character, and character produces hope, and hope does not put us to shame, because God's love has been poured into our hearts through the Holy Spirit who has been given to us" (Romans 5:1, 3–5). Since we've been justified through Christ, we've been saved from God's wrath, and we can rejoice in God through Jesus, who has reconciled us with God.

Basic Bible Teachings

God Gives Us Strength

Living in this world is not always easy. There are so many questions that are difficult to answer, but we know we can turn to God's Word and trust what it says. We know our Lord gives us strength to face this world and promises to be with us always.

Why is there suffering in the world?

In God's Word, we read about a man named Job. He went through a horrible experience and questioned God about it. God answered,

"Where were you when I laid the foundation of the earth? Tell Me, if you have understanding. Who determined its measurements—surely you know!" (Job 38:4-5).

God reminds Job that He is God and we are not. *And that's okay!* It's best that way. We may not need to know why something happened. We may not understand why it happened for a long time—if ever!

With faith like a child, we simply trust that God is our loving **Father** who takes care of us and knows best. We trust Jesus is the Lord of the universe on His throne in heaven, praying for us to His Father (**interceding** on our behalf). Everything is subject to Him. Jesus is the one in control.

Why would God spare some people from suffering, yet others experience tragedy?

Do we really know anyone who has not suffered in this life? Everyone faces the consequences of sin, the suffering, the trials, the temptations, and even death. We may not understand, but we trust that the Lord of the universe who loves us and died for us is in control. And in the midst of sadness and pain, God remains with us and gives us strength to face difficult moments. God did not cause sin or suffering, but God uses His good Law to expose sin, to turn people to Him. He will use suffering to draw us back

© iStock / Aldo Murillo

to Him. By realizing our need for a Savior, God turns sin and suffering into good. He keeps us faithful to Him. This is how the **apostle** Paul could write that even suffering is a blessing from God (Romans 5:3–5).

In the Lord's Prayer, we ask God to "deliver us from evil." We want God to rescue us from the devil and all evil, which has come into the world because of sin. The Lord keeps us from harm and also helps us to make it through the troubles that He allows to come into our lives. We also pray, "Lead us not into temptation." God doesn't tempt us, but God can use temptations to test and strengthen our faith, to bring us closer to Himself. He promises, "My grace is sufficient for you, for My power is made perfect in weakness" (2 Corinthians 12:9).

We have the hope that no matter what sorrows we face here on earth, our Father will take us to Himself in His heavenly kingdom. One day, we will be delivered from sin, suffering, and temptation forever.

> "Oh, the depth of the riches and wisdom and knowledge of God! How unsearchable are His judgments and how inscrutable His ways!" (Romans 11:33)

After suffering, Job realized that God can do all things. God is in control and is working for us in Christ.

After suffering, King David felt like rejoicing. "You have turned for me my mourning into dancing; You have loosed my sackcloth and clothed me with gladness, that my glory may sing Your praise and not be silent" (Psalm 30:11–12). David remembered that for a child of God, suffering here on earth does not last forever. "Weeping may tarry for the night, but joy comes with the morning" (Psalm 30:5).

Why does evil exist?

Philosophers debate why evil exists, and people ask how a good God could allow bad things to happen. But it's not the existence of evil and suffering that requires an explanation; it is the existence of goodness and beauty and love that is most remarkable. A world without God cannot explain such things. The persistence of goodness reminds us of what we have lost since the fall into sin, but it also offers us a glimpse of God's grace and the everlasting **glory** to which God has called us through Christ.

How can we trust anyone?

We have a hard time trusting others. Friends, families, teachers, government officials, employers, and even people at **church** disappoint us. We have expectations for them, and they cannot live up to what we demand. These people and institutions promise to be for us, to support us, and to be with us to the end. But in the end, we can feel alone and abandoned, utterly disappointed and disillusioned. How can we trust anything?

God has never broken any of His promises (Joshua 21:45). God has promised that those who believe in Jesus Christ, who died and rose again to give them eternal life, will be saved from the eternal punishment of their sins. God has promised that He will never leave us or forsake us.

How can we believe these things?

The question here is *who* will we believe? Ourselves, or God? How far can logic take us? How much do we put at stake when trusting only in human reasoning? Can true peace be found within ourselves when we don't know what the future holds? Or is true peace found in trusting an almighty, all-knowing God who already knows the future? True peace is found by trusting an all-loving God who cared enough to save us from sin and eternal death by sending His one and only **Son** from heaven to us on earth.

What if the Bible is wrong? The apostle Paul says: "If Christ has not been raised, your faith is futile and you are still in your sins. Then those also who have fallen asleep in Christ have perished. . . . But in fact Christ has been raised from the dead" (1 Corinthians 15:17–18, 20).

Christ has been raised from the dead. God's promises are all answered through Jesus (2 Corinthians 1:20).

Living with Expectations

In this first chapter, we begin by looking at our place in this world. The world has expectations for us, but we can't quite reach those goals. God has even higher expectations for us, and there is no way we can come close to what He wants for us. Unlike the world, however, God loves us unconditionally and fulfills those expectations *for us*.

God Gives Us Value

When God sees us, He looks at us through His Son. We have value not because of what we do but because of what our Savior Jesus Christ has done *for us*.

Review Romans 6:23. Consider how Jesus changes who we are.

God Gives Us Grace

Grace is a foreign concept to us in this fallen world. Sometimes, we're shocked that God shows us any grace. Other times, we grumble when we see God give free grace to others.

Review Ephesians 2:8–9. Be sure you're familiar with the terms *faith* and *grace*. You'll be seeing those words all the time.

God Gives Us Expectations

Jesus sums up all the Commandments into two main commands. Both of them have to do with putting ourselves and our desires *after* others.

Review Mark 12:30–31. Think about how this mind-set can result in a countercultural lifestyle.

God Gives Us the Law

This section talks about the different ways God uses the Law to show us our sin and lead us to change. It also tackles difficult realities about sin, specifically original sin.

Review Psalm 51:5. Consider how our state as sinners affects our relationship with our holy God.

God Gives Us the Gospel

After we are crushed with the Law, God meets our repentant hearts with the truth of the Gospel. The truth of our salvation in Jesus Christ sets us free! God gives us faith to believe that His promises are true.

Review Romans 5:1, 3–5. Prepare to share how forgiveness in Jesus Christ changes us and how we see the world differently as a result.

God Gives Us Strength

Living the Christian life doesn't mean everything will always go right. In fact, sometimes, it can be even harder to navigate the sinful world as believers. We can trust God to give us strength even when things don't make sense, and we can examine difficult questions in light of His Word.

Review Romans 11:33. Compare God's wisdom with our own.

Living with Expectations

This page serves two purposes. First, it provides questions for you to consider. But it also provides a blank section to store your own questions.

If you're using this book for personal study, this is a great way to record any questions you still have. Then find a time to meet with a pastor, church leader, or church friend to talk things through. **If you meet with a class**, your questions can help fuel great discussion during class time.

Warning: You might need extra writing space.

God Gives Us Value

- How do you evaluate your self-worth? Does your self-perception change when you see yourself as God sees you?
- I can do it! This is often seen as a positive statement in our culture. But how does that cause trouble when it comes to faith? Share experiences of this.
- Look again at the Bible passages offered in this section. What do they say about sin? about you? about God? Highlight one and talk about it.

God Gives Us Grace

- Grace truly is amazing! It's hard for us to comprehend. How might we respond with thankfulness? with doubt? with indignation?
- Take a long look at Matthew 20:1–16. It's a difficult parable for several reasons. Are there parts you don't understand? Are there parts that resonate with you easily?

God Gives Us Expectations

- Jesus summarizes the Commandments with two "new" commandments. They might even be summarized into one word. What word? Why might this be a good word to keep in mind?
- When Christians live according to these commandments, we often baffle those around us. Why?

God Gives Us the Law

- List three ways God uses the Law for our good. Why does God give us the Law?

God Gives Us the Gospel

- The Gospel gives us freedom! It also gives us a new way to see the world. How does a Christian look at life differently in light of the Gospel?

God Gives Us Strength

- This section deals with some tough issues. Do any of these questions hit home with you? Where do you turn for answers?

Your Questions

Try a journal or some large adhesive notes.
TIP

CHAPTER 2
Living with Jesus as Savior

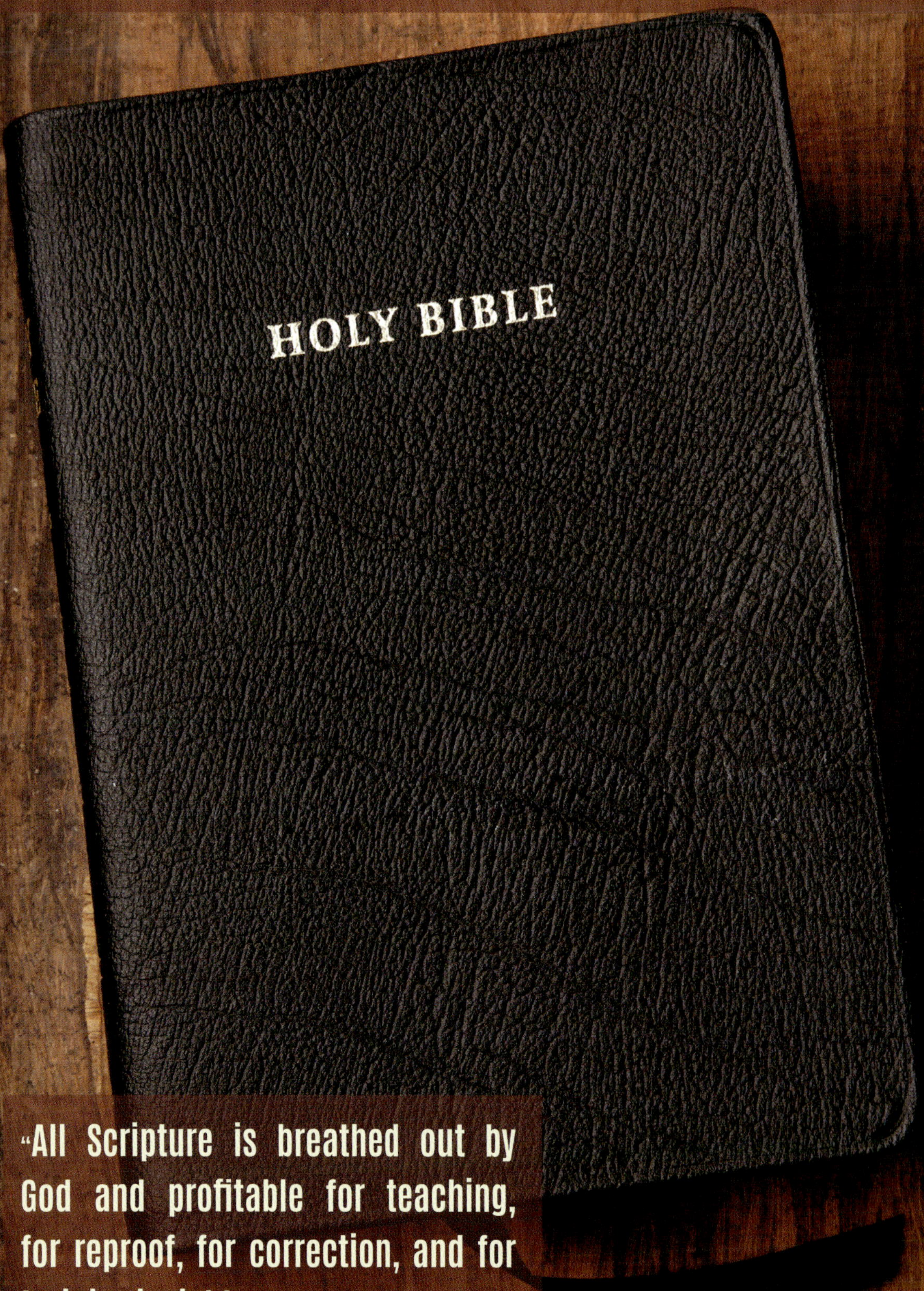

"All Scripture is breathed out by God and profitable for teaching, for reproof, for correction, and for training in righteousness." (2 Timothy 3:16)

God Gives Us His Word

The Bible is the very Word of God and is how we learn about Jesus. The Old Testament is filled with references to the coming Savior (the **Messiah**, Anointed One). From the first story in the Bible (Adam and Eve) and throughout the rest of the accounts, God promises that He will send a Savior to rescue His people.

Old Testament

- Throughout the accounts of God's people in Genesis, we learn that this Savior will be a descendant of Abraham, Isaac, and Jacob.
- Throughout the history of leaders called judges, we learn how God promises to send a Savior to deliver His people from their enemies. When God's people decide they want a king just like the other nations, we learn how God granted them kings, even though their choice didn't put God first in their lives as they rejected Him as their King. God tells them that the Messiah will be from King David's line.
- The **prophets**, who told God's people what God said and preached the Word of God, continually proclaimed God's Law and Gospel to a stubborn and sinful people. Some words of judgment were harsh because God's people had sinned continually by turning to other gods. There were some good kings, but most did not listen to God. The prophets also spoke God's word of promise—the Gospel. They spoke some of the most beautiful, hope-filled messages about a future time of peace and restoration. In these words, the prophets talk about Jesus, who saves us and restores our relationship with God the Father and who will one day come again to restore perfection forever.

New Testament

- We learn much about Jesus from the first four books of the New Testament (the Gospels) because they were written by eyewitnesses who saw Jesus and followed Him as disciples (Matthew and John) or later worked closely with those chosen by Jesus (Luke and Mark). These eyewitnesses detail Jesus' preaching, teaching, and healing ministry, including how He was born, how He lived, and how He died and rose again.
- With the inspiration of the Holy Spirit, the authors wrote to persuade their readers that Jesus is the Christ, God's Son who came to save sinners. The Gospels were written after Jesus ascended to heaven, after He had entrusted His apostles to preach, teach, and baptize all nations. The Book of Acts continues this history, telling how the Church began and how the apostles spread the Good News about Jesus.
- Most of the rest of the New Testament is made up of epistles, or letters, to the early Christian churches and individual Christians. The apostles, chosen by Christ, write about life in Christ's Church. They provide inspiring and encouraging words about the work of the Holy Spirit among them, but they also share cautions about following after worldly desires and arguing among one another. The epistles include great explanations of Jesus' teachings and help us better understand our new life in Him—what Jesus' life, death, and **resurrection** means for our life and salvation. We are "dead to sin and alive to God in Christ Jesus" (Romans 6:11).
- The last book of the New Testament and the final book of the Bible is a prophecy. It describes the visions that were **revealed** to the apostle John.

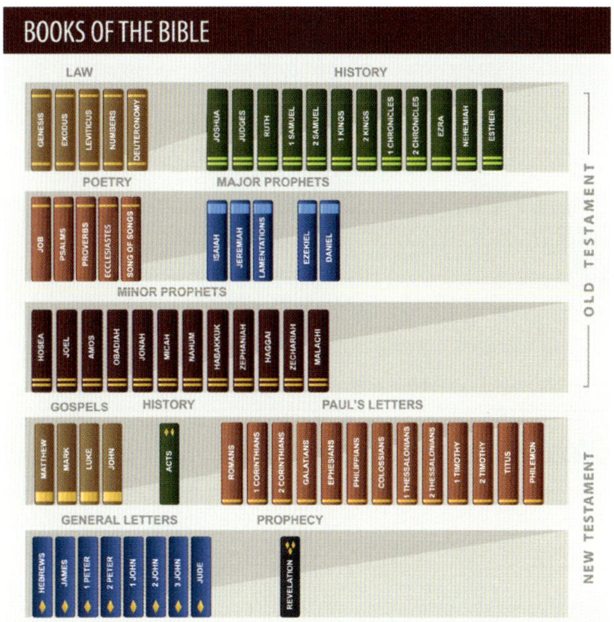

Basic Bible Teachings

God Gives Us Law and Gospel

The Bible is one long narrative about God's plan of salvation, how God loves His people, and the work He did (and does) to bring **repentance** and faith to us. The entire Bible talks about Jesus, your Savior!

The themes of Law and Gospel are communicated throughout the entire Bible. From beginning to end, from Genesis to Revelation, we learn about our sin and punishment, and we learn of God's grace and mercy. We watch God's people struggle (and fail) to remain faithful to God and to love Him above all. And we rejoice in a God that gives His people the **righteousness** of Jesus, both through promise and fulfillment.

After Adam and Eve sinned and fled from the garden, God's people continued to forget they needed God. Through the prophets, the people of God were given the Word of the Lord. Some would hear the accusations of the Law and feel the weight of the effects of sin and repent, recognizing their sin. Others would continue in their sin, rejecting God and His plan of salvation for them.

Always, God forgave those who repented and turned again to Him. Always, God proclaimed through the prophets that a Messiah would come. The Old and New Testament narratives reveal sin and our Savior from sin, Jesus Christ.

Jesus is the center of the Bible because He is the center of our faith. He was there at the beginning, at the creation of the world (John 1:3). He will return on the Last Day to bring all believers in Him to the new heaven and earth, the restored creation. Jesus, the God-man, is the first and the last and everything in between. It is always about Jesus, as it should be, because He is true God.

It is His Law that shows us our sin every day. And He is our Gospel, our Savior, to which we cling every day for forgiveness and the hope of eternal life with Him.

Where is our hope? It is in Christ!

We do not need to fear God's eternal punishment for sin. This is because of the certain hope we have in our Savior Jesus Christ.

"God shows His love for us in that while we were still sinners, Christ died for us" (Romans 5:8). This is the Gospel—Christ died for us. Now, instead of the eternal death we deserve, we receive eternal life with Jesus. Because *Jesus* paid the penalty for *our* sin, we will not have to suffer the punishment and wrath of God that we deserve because of our sins. Instead of being a slave to the power of original sin that drives us to selfishness and evil, we willingly serve a kind and gracious Master, Jesus Christ. Instead of being driven to despair by a guilty **conscience** for secret sins, we are forgiven and can live in joy and confidence. Instead of living apart from God forever, we will live forever with Him in His kingdom, in a perfect, sin-free, new heaven and earth. All this is ours because God has saved us through Jesus.

It is hard to think about the future in these terms. This life doesn't always seem so bad. God **blesses** us with good times with friends and family. Most of us know great joy and happiness in our lives. But we also know fear, disappointment, sadness, shame, and regret.

Christians hope for more than a good life now. A Christian's true hope is the lasting joy and perfection that will be ours eternally when Jesus calls us to our final home with Him. There is more than the life that is before our eyes. This is the hope-filled message for those struggling with illness and disabilities, for those burdened by depression, financial worries, and broken relationships. The Christian message of a perfect eternity with God brings hope to all people, and this hope is centered in Christ. He won salvation and eternal life for us, and He will return to take us to our perfect eternal home. Heaven is the place where believers in Christ will spend eternity in the presence of God Himself.

Dig a Little Deeper

READ Genesis 3 to see how the devil used our pride against us and the consequences of sin.

READ Revelation 22:1–5 to see how Jesus will once and for all restore the perfection that was lost.

God Gives Us Salvation's Story

The Gospel is the Good News that "God so loved the world, that He gave His only Son, that whoever believes in Him should not perish but have eternal life" (John 3:16). God gave His only Son to suffer and die in our place. This act of grace is the only thing that could save us from the penalty of our sin—eternal death. God's grace extends even beyond Christ's sacrificial death. John 3:16 says "whoever believes in Him." And how do we believe? By the power of the Holy Spirit through the Word of God, you are given faith, the very ability to believe in Him who died. Even our faith is a gift. How amazing! God the Father loves us. God the Son died for us. God the Holy Spirit gives us the faith to believe.

True Man

Why did Jesus have to be human? The Law demands perfection. Since we are imperfect and unable to fulfill the Law, Jesus had to take our place. So God sent His Son to earth, to take on human flesh, in order to fulfill (keep) the Law perfectly for us (Matthew 5:17).

Only as a true man could Jesus suffer and die in our place. He became the perfect sacrifice that God demanded to pay for the sin of all people for all time. All humankind belonged to sin and Satan, but Jesus bought us back from sin; He **redeemed** us by paying the penalty that we owed. This is why He is our Redeemer.

True God

Why did Jesus have to be God? Jesus did not become God. From the beginning, Jesus is God. In His **incarnation**, God took on human flesh in the person of Jesus. As the Second Person of the **triune** Godhead, Jesus has all the attributes of God. Through the Holy Spirit, the apostle Paul writes: **"For in [Christ] the whole fullness of deity dwells bodily" (Colossians 2:9)**. And the apostle John records Jesus' own words that He and the Father are one God (John 14:9).

Through the Word of God, we learn how Jesus, true God in human flesh, has the attributes of God.

Jesus is almighty. He has power and authority (Matthew 28:18). There is also power in Jesus' name to do miracles, to heal people, and to raise the dead! In Jesus' name, we are forgiven of our sins. No wonder we often close our **prayers** with the confident words "In Jesus' name we pray. Amen."

Jesus is all-knowing. He knows things only God could know (John 21:17).

He always was and always is; He is eternal. The Bible says that Jesus was there when the world was created. Jesus is called the Word. "In the beginning was the Word, and the Word was with God, and the Word was God. He was in the beginning with God" (John 1:1–2). Jesus said, "I am the Alpha and Omega, the first and the last, the beginning and the end" (Revelation 22:13).

We Learn of Jesus in the Word

Lutherans believe the Bible is God's Word. It's how God speaks to us. Everything we need to know about God is in the Bible. When we learn about Jesus, we are learning about God. When we read about what Jesus did and what He was like, we see what God is like. Jesus said, "Whoever has seen Me has seen the Father" (John 14:9). God is love, and the more we read the Bible, the more we get to know who He is and see that everything He does is for our good, because we are His people.

WHAT IS THE BIBLE?

We call it the Holy Scriptures because God the Holy Spirit told the people who wrote the Bible what words to use. The Bible is **inspired** by the Holy Spirit: **"All Scripture is breathed out by God" (2 Timothy 3:16)**. The Holy Spirit comes to us through God's Word to deliver His gifts of repentance and faith to us. The Holy Spirit always points us to Jesus, who is the Word of God.

Since the Bible is God's own words, it is perfect (holy). There is nothing wrong with it—there are no errors. We don't add anything to it or take anything away from it. **Pastors** learn Hebrew (the language of the Old Testament) and Greek (the language of the New Testament) so that they can read God's Word as it was originally written.

The Bible is best understood by letting the context and the rest of Scripture explain Scripture. This means we consider the context of the Bible passages and accounts. We consider the audience, the background, and the message. We look to other places in the Bible to help us clarify and understand what is being taught. The Bible is the only source for what we believe. Everything else is judged by comparing it to the Scriptures.

The Bible is living and active (Hebrews 4:12). When you read it, you can trust that you are hearing and reading the very Word of God, which is "the power of God for salvation" (Romans 1:16). Through the Word of God, the Holy Spirit is at work in your heart. God uses it to accomplish His purpose (Isaiah 55:1–11), which is to give and to strengthen your faith. This faith "comes from hearing, and hearing through the word of Christ" (Romans 10:17).

In the Bible, we see short statements of faith by believers in Jesus:

- Paul writes in Romans 10:9, "If you confess with your mouth that Jesus is Lord and believe in your heart that God raised Him from the dead, you will be saved."
- Thomas said, "My Lord and my God!" (John 20:28).
- Peter said, "You are the Christ, the Son of the living God" (Matthew 16:16).
- In Peter's speech found in Acts 10:34–43, he summarizes Jesus' three years of ministry here on earth: "God anointed Jesus of Nazareth with the Holy Spirit and with power. He went about doing good and healing all who were oppressed by the devil, for God was with Him. And we are witnesses of all that He did both in the country of the Jews and in Jerusalem. They put Him to death by hanging Him on a tree, but God raised Him on the third day and made Him to appear, not to all the people but to us who had been chosen by God as witnesses, who ate and drank with Him after He rose from the dead. And He commanded us to preach to the people and to testify that He is the one appointed by God to be judge of the living and the dead. To Him all the prophets bear witness that everyone who believes in Him receives forgiveness of sins through His name" (vv. 38–43).

God Gives Us Faith

A **creed** is a statement of what we believe, teach, and confess. It is the statement of your faith, and your faith comes from and clings to the words of Christ: "Faith comes from hearing, and hearing through the word of Christ" (Romans 10:17).

Your creed, your statement of faith, is personal because it reflects what you believe. It is also personal because no one can be saved by another person's faith. When you say you believe in God, you are saying that *you* trust His promises and consider the Bible all true. A creed is also special because it's something shared with all other true believers in God.

The Apostles' Creed is important because it summarizes what we believe. The apostles (Jesus' original disciples and Paul, the first leaders of the Christian Church, chosen by Him to preach the Gospel) did not write the words of this creed, but it states what God gave us through the teachings of the apostles in the Bible. The apostles were the first to proclaim the fullness of the triune God: the Father, Son, and Holy Spirit.

The *ICHTHUS* was an early symbol for Jesus.

Before the Apostles' Creed, the Early Christians had a simple statement of faith. Under severe persecution, they confessed and shared their faith by using the symbol of the fish (*ICHTHUS*). This was the symbol for Jesus. The letters of the Greek word for "fish" stand for "Jesus Christ, God's Son, Savior." While much simpler than the Apostles' Creed, the **confession** is the same. Jesus Christ, God's Son, is our Savior. To better understand that statement, you simply need to reflect on the Apostles' Creed. Both emphasize that the center of our faith, the center of our confession, is Jesus Christ, true God and true man.

Jesus Christ is the center of our faith because God has made Him so. The Bible teaches us that from the promise made by God to Adam and Eve until the Last Day, God's perfect plan of salvation—of restoring His people to Him—has centered on the person and work of Jesus Christ. He alone would come to suffer, die, and rise again for all humankind, just as God promised and just as God fulfilled. He alone would make everything right between us and the Father, so that eternal life in His name may be given to those who believe in Him (John 3:16). From the beginning, God created us to be in a perfect relationship with Him eternally. Through Christ alone, this restoration is accomplished by God's grace through faith.

What is faith? Faith is believing in Jesus Christ as your Savior. Lutherans use the phrase "faith alone" because it reminds us to always go back to the center of our faith—Jesus Christ. In this life, we will continue to want to do something to earn our salvation. Remember, it just doesn't make sense that Jesus did everything for us. By saying that we are saved through Christ alone by faith alone, we avoid adding our **good works**, love, enthusiasm, or attitudes into the salvation equation. Christ alone! Faith alone! And there is even more good news: "For by grace you have been saved through faith. And this is not your own doing; it is the gift of God, not a result of works, so that no one may boast" (Ephesians 2:8–9).

Faith is a gift, given through the Holy Spirit! We cannot make things right with God by trying to please God with what we do. Only Jesus can restore perfection. Lutherans call this restoration **justification**. Justification means that our relationship with God is back to the way it was before humans ever sinned, "just as if" sin had never happened. We are innocent. We are holy (righteous) once again. The only way this is possible is through Jesus' death and resurrection. God has reconciled us to Himself through Jesus. The Holy Spirit gives us faith to believe this.

The First Article

Creation

I believe in God, the Father Almighty, Maker of heaven and earth.

What does this mean? I believe that God has made me and all creatures; that He has given me my body and soul, eyes, ears, and all my members, my reason and all my senses, and still takes care of them.

He also gives me clothing and shoes, food and drink, house and home, wife and children, land, animals, and all I have. He richly and daily provides me with all that I need to support this body and life.

He defends me against all danger and guards and protects me from all evil.

All this He does only out of fatherly, divine goodness and mercy, without any merit or worthiness in me. For all this it is my duty to thank and praise, serve and obey Him.

This is most certainly true.

The Second Article

Redemption

And in Jesus Christ, His only Son, our Lord, who was conceived by the Holy Spirit, born of the Virgin Mary, suffered under Pontius Pilate, was crucified, died and was buried. He descended into hell. The third day He rose again from the dead. He ascended into heaven and sits at the right hand of God, the Father Almighty. From thence He will come to judge the living and the dead.

What does this mean? I believe that Jesus Christ, true God, begotten of the Father from eternity, and also true man, born of the Virgin Mary, is my Lord, who has redeemed me, a lost and condemned person, purchased and won me from all sins, from death, and from the power of the devil; not with gold or silver, but with His holy, precious blood and with His innocent suffering and death, that I may be His own and live under Him in His kingdom and serve Him in everlasting righteousness, innocence, and blessedness, just as He is risen from the dead, lives and reigns to all eternity.

This is most certainly true.

The Third Article

Sanctification

I believe in the Holy Spirit, the holy Christian church, the communion of saints, the forgiveness of sins, the resurrection of the body, and the life everlasting. Amen.

What does this mean? I believe that I cannot by my own reason or strength believe in Jesus Christ, my Lord, or come to Him; but the Holy Spirit has called me by the Gospel, enlightened me with His gifts, sanctified and kept me in the true faith.

In the same way He calls, gathers, enlightens, and sanctifies the whole Christian church on earth, and keeps it with Jesus Christ in the one true faith.

In this Christian church He daily and richly forgives all my sins and the sins of all believers.

On the Last Day He will raise me and all the dead, and give eternal life to me and all believers in Christ.

This is most certainly true.

God Gives Us Righteousness

Faith is given to you. Through the Word of God, the Holy Spirit begins His work in you. For the first time, you may hear God's Law and recognize yourself as a sinner. This is the Holy Spirit working repentance in you and is the very first sign of the faith He has delivered to you. The Holy Spirit continues His work through the Gospel, giving you forgiveness of sins and eternal life through Jesus.

Lutherans believe a person is given faith by the grace and power of God alone working through His Word. The Holy Spirit is God at work, not *us*. We cannot change our own hearts, open them up, or make a decision to follow Christ. By our own understanding or effort, we can't believe in Jesus or come to Him. The Holy Spirit calls us to faith through the Word of God.

What a relief to leave it all in the Lord's hands! **Conversion** is a work of the Holy Spirit through the Gospel. "No one can say 'Jesus is Lord' except in the Holy Spirit" (1 Corinthians 12:3).

If you know of someone who doesn't yet believe, you can have comfort knowing that God desires that everyone would come to saving faith and that He does not leave this work to us. People can and will continue to resist the Holy Spirit and reject the Gospel, but it is God's will (desire) that "all should reach repentance" (2 Peter 3:9) and live with Him in His heavenly kingdom forever. We leave God's work to Him, trusting in Him to deliver His Word and faith to those who need it. We may serve as His hands, feet, and mouthpieces to deliver the Word of God, but the saving work all belongs to God, when and where He wills.

God becoming a human, God humbling Himself to suffer and die in our place, God giving us the gift of faith . . . it's hard for our human minds to understand! And that's the point. On our own, we can't and wouldn't naturally believe what God tells us. Who He is, what He's done for us, and what He's continuing to do in our lives and in the future is incomprehensible for our limited understanding. Thankfully, whenever we read or hear God's Word, the Holy Spirit is at work.

God called undeserving Matthew, a tax collector. God called Peter, a fisherman. "When [people] saw the boldness of Peter and John, and perceived that they were uneducated, common men, they were astonished. And they recognized that they had been with Jesus" (Acts 4:13).

In Christ alone, our sins are removed once and for all. "In Him [Jesus] we have redemption through His blood, the forgiveness of our trespasses, according to the riches of His grace" (Ephesians 1:7). Jesus is called the "Lamb of God" because He sacrificed Himself on the cross in order to *pay off the debt of our sins*. Because of our sin against God, a payment for that sin was owed to Him. Jesus gave His life as payment for our sin. He is our Redeemer, who bought us back with His blood from the power of sin, death, and the devil.

Jesus is the atoning sacrifice for the sins of all people (1 John 2:2); He has made amends with God, and like a debt that has been paid, everything is reconciled. There is no balance due—nothing more we need do.

God's anger toward us because of sin is satisfied through Jesus, so God is not angry at us. We are guilty of sinning, but because of Jesus, God doesn't look at us that way. Because Jesus bore the guilt and punishment, we have been declared not guilty. This status changes everything.

We no longer live in fear of God's wrath. We no longer live as God's enemies. We are free to serve Him and love Him with our whole heart, **soul**, and mind and to love our neighbors as ourselves. Because of Jesus, God is approachable again! We are justified by grace, for Christ's sake, through faith.

Names of Jesus

Advocate (1 John 2:1)

Almighty (Matthew 28:18; Revelation 1:8)

Alpha and Omega (Revelation 22:13)

Amen (Revelation 3:14)

Apostle and High Priest of our confession (Hebrews 3:1)

Author of life (Acts 3:15)

Beginning and end (Revelation 22:13)

Beginning of God's creation (Revelation 3:14)

Blessed and only Sovereign (1 Timothy 6:15)

Bread of God (John 6:33)

Bread of life (John 6:35, 48)

Bridegroom (Matthew 25:1)

Chief Shepherd (1 Peter 5:4)

Christ (1 John 2:22)

Cornerstone (Acts 4:11; Ephesians 2:20; 1 Peter 2:7)

Deliverer (Romans 11:26)

Descendant of David (Revelation 22:16)

Door (John 10:9)

Eternal life (1 John 1:2; 5:20)

Faithful and True (Revelation 19:11)

Faithful and true witness (Revelation 3:14)

First and last (Revelation 1:17; 2:8; 22:13)

Firstborn of all creation (Colossians 1:15)

Firstborn of the dead (Revelation 1:5)

Founder and perfecter of our faith (Hebrews 12:2)

Founder of salvation (Hebrews 2:10)

God (John 1:1; Romans 9:5; 2 Peter 1:1; 1 John 5:20; etc.)

Good Shepherd (John 10:11, 14)

Great High Priest (Hebrews 4:14)

Great Shepherd (Hebrews 13:20)

Head of the Church (Ephesians 5:23)

Heir of all things (Hebrews 1:2)

High Priest (Hebrews 2:17)

Holy and Righteous One (Acts 3:14)

Holy and true (Revelation 3:7)

Hope (1 Timothy 1:1)

Hope of glory (Colossians 1:27)

Horn of salvation (Luke 1:69)

I Am (John 8:58)

Image of God (2 Corinthians 4:4)

Immanuel (Matthew 1:23)

Judge of the living and the dead (Acts 10:42)

King of ages (1 Timothy 1:17)

King of Israel (John 1:49)

King of the Jews (Matthew 27:11)

King of kings (1 Timothy 6:15; Revelation 19:16)

King of the nations (Revelation 15:3)

Lamb (Revelation 13:8)

Lamb of God (John 1:29)

Lamb without blemish (1 Peter 1:19)

Last Adam (1 Corinthians 15:45)

Life (John 14:6; Colossians 3:4)

Light of the world (John 8:12)

Lion of the tribe of Judah (Revelation 5:5)

© iStock / Peter Zelei

Living one (Revelation 1:18)

Living stone (1 Peter 2:4)

Lord (2 Peter 2:20)

Lord of all (Acts 10:36)

Lord of glory (1 Corinthians 2:8)

Lord of lords (1 Timothy 6:15; Revelation 19:16)

Man of heaven (1 Corinthians 15:48)

Master (Luke 5:5; 8:24)

Mediator of a new covenant (Hebrews 9:15)

Mighty God (Isaiah 9:6)

Morning star (Revelation 22:16)

Only Son of God (1 John 4:9)

Our great God and Savior (Titus 2:13)

Our Guard (2 Thessalonians 3:3)

Our Husband (2 Corinthians 11:2)

Our Passover Lamb (1 Corinthians 5:7)

Our Redemption (1 Corinthians 1:30)

Our Righteousness (1 Corinthians 1:30)

Our Sanctification (1 Corinthians 1:30)

Power of God (1 Corinthians 1:24)

Precious cornerstone (1 Peter 2:6)

Prince of Peace (Isaiah 9:6)

Prophet (Acts 3:22)

Propitiation for our sins (1 John 2:2)

Rabbi (Matthew 26:25)

Resurrection and life (John 11:25)

Righteous Branch (Jeremiah 23:5)

Righteous One (Acts 7:52; 1 John 2:1)

Rock (1 Corinthians 10:4)

Root of David (Revelation 5:5; 22:16)

Savior (Ephesians 5:23; Titus 1:4; 3:6; 2 Peter 2:20)

Son of David (Luke 18:39)

Son of God (John 1:49; Hebrews 4:14)

Son of Man (Matthew 8:20)

Son of the Most High (Luke 1:32)

Source of eternal salvation to all who obey Him (Hebrews 5:9)

The one mediator (1 Timothy 2:5)

The stone the builders rejected (Acts 4:11)

True bread from heaven (John 6:32)

True light (John 1:9)

True vine (John 15:1)

Truth (John 1:14; 14:6)

Way (John 14:6)

Wisdom of God (1 Corinthians 1:24)

Word (John 1:1)

Word of God (Revelation 19:13)

Living with Jesus as Savior

In this chapter, we see how Jesus is the center of everything. He is the center of the Bible, the center of our faith, the center of God's plan for our salvation.

God Gives Us His Word

Take a look at the different sections of the Bible, the different types of Bible books. What experience do you have with these parts? Which sections would you like to explore more?

Review 2 Timothy 3:16. Think about how you usually approach God's Word.

God Gives Us Law and Gospel

Both Law and Gospel are essential to our understanding of our relationship with God. If these concepts are still confusing, take some time to understand both Law and Gospel and how they work together. Remember that Law shows our sin and Gospel shows our Savior.

Review Romans 5:8. Where is the Law in this passage? Where is the Gospel?

God Gives Us Salvation's Story

The Bible tells of Jesus, our Savior. By studying God's Word, we learn more of Jesus. When we learn more of Jesus, we discover how deeply God loves us in sending His Son to die for us. We learn that Jesus, true God and true man, was the perfect substitute for the punishment we deserve.

Review Acts 10:34–43. Consider writing a summary in your own words of who Jesus is and what He does.

God Gives Us Faith

The Holy Spirit gives us faith in our Savior Jesus Christ. Because we believe in Jesus, the Son of God, we are forgiven and saved from our sins. We are made right with God the Father, and we will enjoy eternal life with Him. God uses His people to spread His Word to others, that the Holy Spirit will work in their hearts and give them faith as well.

Review Romans 10:17. Consider the importance of God's Word when it comes to reaching out to unbelievers.

God Gives Us Righteousness

Because of Jesus, we are made holy. Because of who He is, we are made children of God. We are now free to serve the Lord not out of obligation but in joy and thankfulness.

Review 1 Corinthians 12:3. Consider how important the Holy Spirit is to faith in Christ.

Living with Jesus as Savior

This page serves two purposes. First, it provides questions for you to consider. But it also provides a blank section to store your own questions.

If you're using this book for personal study, this is a great way to record any questions you still have. Then find a time to meet with a pastor, church leader, or church friend to talk things through. **If you meet with a class**, your questions can help fuel great discussion during class time.

Warning: You might need extra writing space.

God Gives Us His Word

- Lutheran Christians believe that the Bible is the very Word of God, without error. How does this affect the way we use the Bible?

- Think about those who do not view the Bible as God's Word. How does this affect the way they talk about God? Share personal examples, if you feel comfortable.

God Gives Us Law and Gospel

- Why is the Law important to our faith?

- Why is the Gospel important to our faith?

God Gives Us Salvation's Story

- God's Word is centered on Jesus. Why is a Christ-centered approach to reading God's Word important? In other words, why does Jesus matter so much?

- Jesus is true God and true man. Take some time to think about this amazing mystery. Why does Jesus need to be both?

God Gives Us Faith

- Faith is a gift. A gift! How does this affect your perception of your status as a "believer"? How does it affect the way you reach out to others with God's Word?

God Gives Us Righteousness

- When God sees us, He now sees Jesus. What does that mean?

- Look at some of the names of Jesus. What do those names say about who He is? What do they say about what He has done for us?

Your Questions

Try a journal or some large adhesive notes.

TIP

CHAPTER 3

Living as God's Child

The Son of God has redeemed us. Now, we are children of God, heirs of heaven and loved by our heavenly Father. We are part of God's family. But how does that happen? These words seem simple enough, but the concepts can be very difficult to understand. How does an almighty God become "Dad"? It's part of the beautiful mystery of grace, and it's a large part of what this chapter will address.

If all of these spiritual concepts (such as righteousness, grace, and justification) are too difficult to understand by our own reason, then how do we "get" faith? How can we believe that Jesus is the truth and that God keeps all His promises? The means, or way, in which God gives us the gift of faith is something so simple—water—and something so powerful—His Word. It is God the Holy Spirit who creates faith in us through God's Word and baptizing. **Baptism** is called a **Means of Grace** because it's the manner or method by which God gives us the forgiveness, life, and salvation won by Jesus' death and resurrection.

> **"Whoever believes and is baptized will be saved, but whoever does not believe will be condemned."** (Mark 16:16)

Baptizing means to apply water on someone (through pouring, washing, dunking, and so on). But Baptism was commanded by God (Matthew 28:19), so it is water included in God's command and combined with God's Word. It is water that washes away our filthy sin and makes us clean.

Because Baptism

- was commanded (instituted/established) by God,
- uses God's Word and something physical/visible (water),
- and gives forgiveness of sins through Christ,

it is called a **sacrament** (a holy, or **sacred**, act).

God instructs Baptism to be done to "all nations" (Matthew 28:19). All people, young and old, including babies, are to be baptized. Everyone has sinned. The psalmist says, "In sin did my mother conceive me" (Psalm 51:5). Peter phrased it,

> **"Repent and be baptized every one of you"** (Acts 2:38).

Jesus told Nicodemus, "Unless one is born of water and the Spirit, he cannot enter the kingdom of God" (John 3:5). That includes all people. As Christians, we don't want to withhold this wonderful gift of God from anyone because of age or any other superficial reason.

God Gives Us New Life

© iStock / Jason Doiy

Through Baptism, God receives us into **fellowship** with Himself!

- God the Father adopts us as His children and gives us the riches of His inheritance, His heavenly home. We become members of His kingdom.
- God makes a promise to us that we will be His forever.
- God the Son washes away our sins. That means our sins are forgiven (Acts 2:38). Jesus rescues us from death and the devil.
- Our Baptism into Christ unites us with Him in a death like His, but also in a resurrection like His (Romans 6:3–5)!
- Through Baptism, we are made holy because our sins are gone. We are clothed with Christ (Galatians 3:27); His righteousness is ours, giving us eternal salvation.
- Jesus is with us, and will be forever (Ephesians 4:4–6).
- The Holy Spirit gives us faith in this Good News. Our lives are renewed.

What does it mean to be **born again** by the Spirit? Our sinful nature has been drowned. Jesus has buried our sin and given us new life in Him. We are new creations. Each day we put on a new self, "created after the likeness of God in true righteousness and holiness" (Ephesians 4:24).

Clearly, Baptism is important. Yes, it is a command of God (Matthew 28:19). But it's vital to remember that it is a *gift* of God. We can be thankful that God gave us Baptism and promises the Holy Spirit and rescue and forgiveness in this Sacrament. What if you're not baptized? There is a careful balance when discussing Baptism and salvation.

Our answers come from the Bible. Jesus said, "I am the way, and the truth, and the life. No one comes to the Father except through Me" (John 14:6). Faith in Jesus is the only way to eternal life. Those who do not believe in their Savior are not saved from their sins. "Repent and be baptized every one of you in the name of Jesus Christ for the forgiveness of your sins, and you will receive the gift of the Holy Spirit" (Acts 2:38). The "best-case scenario" is faith and Baptism. When we see the amazing benefits promised in Baptism (see again the earlier list), we may ask ourselves, *Why would I* not *be baptized?*

For those who have heard God's Word and believe in Jesus, yet die before they were able to be baptized, we trust in the promises of God, who has promised to give eternal life to all who believe in Jesus.

> **"He gave His only Son, that whoever believes in Him should not perish but have eternal life."**
> (John 3:16)

How is a person saved from eternal punishment? By believing in Jesus! Jesus suffered, died, and rose again to save all humankind from sin and eternal death. By faith, we believe this. Plain and simple faith.

There is simplicity to our faith because we depend entirely on God's mercy for forgiveness. Like a baby, we are helpless to do anything at all to become worthy before God and earn salvation.

The Sacrament of Holy Baptism

First

What is Baptism?

Baptism is not just plain water, but it is the water included in God's command and combined with God's word.

Which is that word of God?

Christ our Lord says in the last chapter of Matthew: "Therefore go and make disciples of all nations, baptizing them in the name of the Father and of the Son and of the Holy Spirit." (Matt. 28:19)

Second

What benefits does Baptism give?

It works forgiveness of sins, rescues from death and the devil, and gives eternal salvation to all who believe this, as the words and promises of God declare.

Which are these words and promises of God?

Christ our Lord says in the last chapter of Mark: "Whoever believes and is baptized will be saved, but whoever does not believe will be condemned." (Mark 16:16)

Third

How can water do such great things?

Certainly not just water, but the word of God in and with the water does these things, along with the faith which trusts this word of God in the water. For without God's word the water is plain water and no Baptism. But with the word of God it is a Baptism, that is, a life-giving water, rich in grace, and a washing of the new birth in the Holy Spirit, as St. Paul says in Titus, chapter three:

"He saved us through the washing of rebirth and renewal by the Holy Spirit, whom He poured out on us generously through Jesus Christ our Savior, so that, having been justified by His grace, we might become heirs having the hope of eternal life. This is a trustworthy saying." (Titus 3:5–8)

Fourth

What does such baptizing with water indicate?

It indicates that the Old Adam in us should by daily contrition and repentance be drowned and die with all sins and evil desires, and that a new man should daily emerge and arise to live before God in righteousness and purity forever.

Where is this written?

St. Paul writes in Romans chapter six: "We were therefore buried with Him through baptism into death in order that, just as Christ was raised from the dead through the glory of the Father, we too may live a new life." (Rom. 6:4)

I don't have to understand it first?

The focus is always on what *God* does for *us*. In Baptism, God chooses the person and calls him or her to be His own and live in His kingdom. It's not a decision we make to know when it's the "right time" to be baptized. God is always the one in control and always the one who initiates things. The Holy Spirit creates faith; we don't. It's a good thing that it's not up to us to make such decisions!

Even babies are sinful and have a sinful nature and need their sins washed away. Babies can't understand great theological truths, but the Holy Spirit gives faith to them because they are sinners. It is what *God* knows about us, not what *we* know about God, that makes Baptism such a special act of God.

The Blessing of Sponsors

The Church encourages **sponsors** at Baptism. These people promise to pray for the child who is baptized and to help in raising him or her in the Christian faith. Often, when children are older, they go through the Rite of **Confirmation**, when they publicly make confession of their faith, reaffirming their baptismal vows in their own voices.

God Gives Us a Name

During Holy Baptism, the pastor asks, "How are you named?" This is special, but there is another name that is important in Baptism. This name is essential to Christian Baptism. Jesus commands us to baptize "in the name of the Father and of the Son and of the Holy Spirit" (Matthew 28:19). This is the name of our triune God.

And here is another mystery we believe in faith: the triune God—Father, Son, and Holy Spirit. Three distinct persons in one divine (holy) being. Our human minds just can't grasp the nature and fullness of a triune God, but He has revealed to us all we need to know about Him. He does this in language we can understand and comprehend. Through God's Word, we know God by learning what He says about Himself and the work He does for us. His greatness is a comfort to us!

God tells us He is one God with three distinct persons within the Godhead:

© iStock / Pam Schodt

- God the Father created us.
- God the Son redeemed us.
- God the Holy Spirit sanctifies us (makes us holy).

Yet, the Bible says God is one. Through all the works of God—creating, redeeming, sanctifying—the one God is present.

Thankfully, faith is a gift from God that doesn't rely on our own reason to explain God. We do not have to completely understand God to know He exists, to understand His work, and to respond in faith with love and trust in this God.

By faith, we simply trust in our almighty God to take care of us. Because of sin, we can't figure things out on our own. We humbly trust that He is capable of knowing all our needs, capable of providing for all our needs, and loving enough to care for all our needs, as any loving father does for his child.

"Whoever humbles himself like this child is the greatest in the kingdom of heaven."
(Matthew 18:4)

Children must rely on their parents to take care of them. Children look to their parents for food, shelter, clothing, and also for nurture and love. For most parents, taking care of their children with love, training, discipline, food, clothing, and shelter becomes their highest priority.

Who Am I?

Without faith in God the Father, Creator of heaven and earth, humans question where they came from and why they're here. Human reason alone can't provide an answer.

But *with* faith in God the Father, Creator of heaven and earth, there is a peace in knowing that He made us. We are not an accident of nature, but we were intricately formed as a potter forms clay. God thought of every detail. We were created uniquely. Everyone is different. Because God created you, you are special to God!

Basic Bible Teachings

God Gives Us What We Need

Though still tainted by sin, parents love their children despite their children's faults, lack of thankfulness, and constant demands. How much more does our loving heavenly Father love and provide for us as His children?

- God is perfect. God never makes mistakes when it comes to taking care of you.
- God is all-knowing. He knows exactly what we need and when we need it.
- God is all-powerful. There is nothing He can't do for us, and He knows what is best for us.
- God is present everywhere. He is always there for you.
- God is eternal and unchanging. His love never runs out. His mercies are new every morning; we don't have to wonder what "mood" He's in. We don't have to wonder if He'll still be there in the future. He will never leave us or forsake us.

We are created beings, not gods. We are not independent and self-sufficient beings. Creatures are dependent on their Creator. We are dependent on God, who gives us all good things. "What do you have that you did not receive?" (1 Corinthians 4:7). We can trust that God will take better care of us than we can imagine. "Every good and every perfect gift is from above, coming down from the Father of lights" (James 1:17).

We are interconnected and interdependent with God's creation and His other creatures. We need water, food, and shelter. We need love from others. We are not able to survive without anyone or anything else. God created us within a community and supplies our daily needs through the labor of others. He gives us families to love and nurture us. All these gifts He gives to believers and unbelievers. This is His great goodness to all humankind.

With faith in God the Father, we know why God created us. We are His beloved creation, His special workmanship, His masterpiece. The first story in the Bible tells us that God made the world for us. Humans were the last thing God created—the grand finale. We are His prized creation. He gave us dominion over the rest of His creation. Humans are to take care of the world. "The Lord God took the man and put him in the garden of Eden to work it and keep it" (Genesis 2:15). God brought all the animals to man to see what he would call them (Genesis 2:19).

We were created to **worship** God and bring Him glory. The apostle Paul urges us, "Whatever you do, do all to the glory of God" (1 Corinthians 10:31). It's what our revived

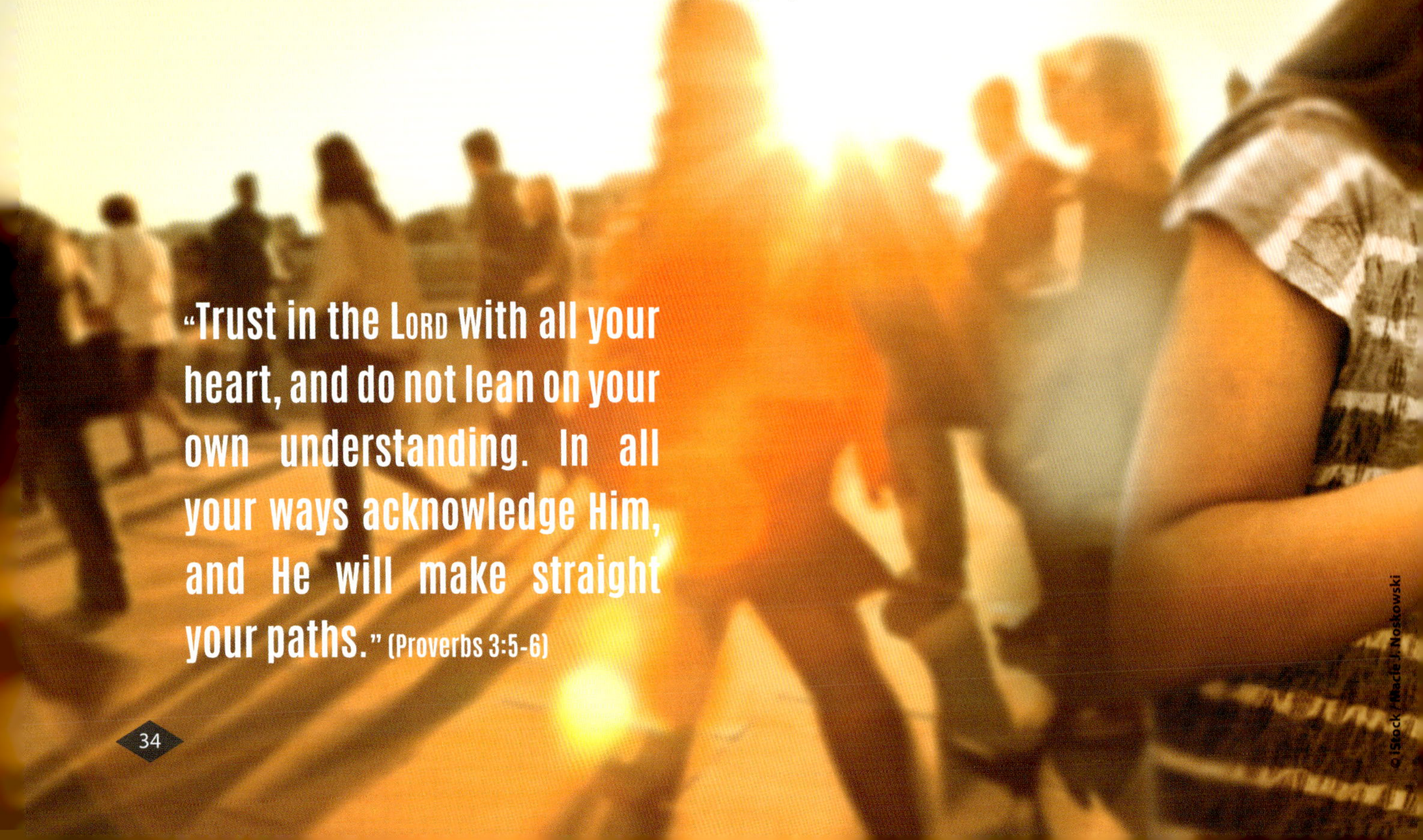

"Trust in the Lord with all your heart, and do not lean on your own understanding. In all your ways acknowledge Him, and He will make straight your paths." (Proverbs 3:5-6)

souls desire to do, and we find satisfaction in being with God, receiving His gifts through His Word and Sacraments (Psalm 27:4). Our Creator and Lord is due the highest honor and praise (Revelation 4:11).

God provides, preserves, and protects.

We couldn't live without God. "As a deer pants for flowing streams, so pants my soul for You, O God. My soul thirsts for God, for the living God" (Psalm 42:1–2). The universe depends on God. Every created thing—human, plant, animal, solar system—needs God to supply its physical needs. God maintains the world and its resources; He is in control. God commands His angels to protect us from danger.

But God supplies us with more than our physical needs. He provides for our spiritual needs as well. Without God, we would be parched, wither away, and die. Through Word and Sacrament, God fills our weary souls with everything we need spiritually. We can trust our loving God to give us all we need.

"You open Your hand; You satisfy the desire of every living thing."
(Psalm 145:16)

Dig a Little Deeper

READ Mark 10:13–16 to hear how Jesus welcomes little children and babies to Himself.

READ John 3:1–15, where Nicodemus asked Jesus questions about faith.

"So God created man in His own image, in the image of God He created him; male and female He created them."
(Genesis 1:27)

God Gives Us Peace

How can we have peace when there is so much that could happen to us? A quick look at the news reveals all the threats that surround us: natural disasters, war, accidents, incurable diseases, and violence. Even though God is in control, these things still happen as consequences of sin.

The weight of the Law moves us to lay the burden of our personal sins at the foot of the cross. The comfort of the Gospel reminds us that God loves us and will care for us, even amidst the sin and danger of this world. All this He does out of fatherly, divine goodness and mercy. God loves us and sustains us with His grace.

God is our protector. In the Book of Psalms, God is described as a refuge and fortress. His faithfulness is a shield. The problems associated with sin will affect us, but "he who dwells in the shelter of the Most High will abide in the shadow of the Almighty" (Psalm 91:1). He covers us to shelter us, and He delivers us from evil.

"[Cast] all your anxieties on Him, because He cares for you." (1 Peter 5:7)

All things are God's. He owns and has rights to everything. All that we have is His. This is truly a good thing! It's best that He "has the whole world in His hands," for in our own hands, the world becomes a messy, chaotic place. We trust His care and **providence**, even when it doesn't make sense or isn't on our own timeline. We sin when we expect God to deliver what we want when we want it. Through the Holy Spirit, we repent of this and the doubt and worry that pull us away from trusting in God, His schedule, and His care for us.

> "[God] has blessed us in Christ with every spiritual blessing in the heavenly places, even as He chose us in Him before the foundation of the world, that we should be holy and blameless before Him. In love He predestined us for adoption as sons through Jesus Christ, according to the purpose of His will." (Ephesians 1:3–5)

Before God laid the foundation of the world, He chose you to be His. In eternity, this time before anything was, a time we don't understand, God was thinking about you!

Before you could even do anything good (thinking you can earn His favor) or anything bad (thinking you can lose His love), He loved you! This is the ultimate example to show you that it's not about what you do. It's all about your identity as God's beloved creation, His beloved child!

"Do not be anxious about your life, what you will eat or what you will drink, nor about your body, what you will put on. . . . Which of you by being anxious can add a single hour to his span of life?" (Matthew 6:25, 27)

God Gives Us Free Will

Before the foundation of the world, God had a marvelous plan, that all people would live with Him forever. Out of nothing, He brought forth all that is in our vast universe. He formed the first man with His own hands. He created Adam and Eve in His **image** and gave them free will. Adam and Eve exercised this free will and chose sin instead of loving obedience to God. But God, in His **omniscience**, knew of this and had a plan: His plan for our redemption in Jesus.

Some people blame God for Adam and Eve's fall into sin. They say He shouldn't have placed the tree in the garden. But God did not create us to be robots or puppets. He does not force us to love Him.

It is God's will that all people would be with Him forever. We messed up His plan. With Adam and Eve, we are sinners who deserve death. Because of Jesus, we will be with God again. Jesus tells us, "I give them eternal life, and they will never perish, and no one will snatch them out of My hand" (John 10:28).

Through Christ, our **reconciliation** to God is complete. This is called **atonement**; Christ paid for the sins of all people of all time. It is God's will that all be saved, that none die an eternal death. He gives the gift of faith through His Word and Holy Baptism. In Baptism, our status before God changes from enemy of God to child of God.

In Baptism, God makes us His own and puts His name on us. In fact, the names of those in Christ are written in the Book of Life (Revelation 14:1; 3:5). God tells us, "Behold, I have engraved you on the palms of My hands" (Isaiah 49:16). Knowing that our sins are forgiven gives us a peace that nothing else can give.

Nothing can separate us from the love of God that is ours through Jesus (Romans 8:38–39). God will always love us, but we have the power to deny His salvation. In disbelief and sin, we can separate ourselves from God, rejecting His Word and His gifts, such as Baptism. Even though Christ atoned for all sins on the cross, unbelievers remain in sin, rejecting the forgiveness won for them and delivered through the Means of Grace (God's Word, Holy Baptism, and Holy **Communion**).

Why do some people reject such good gifts? We can still exercise our free will to reject God. Sadly, our free will only goes one way. We have power to reject God and His salvation. However, the ability to choose *God* is not a choice we possess.

The good news is the Holy Spirit works in us to do what we cannot. By His power working through God's Word and Baptism, He brings us to recognize God's truth for us—that we are sinners and that we have a Savior. We respond in gratitude for His blessings! We obey and serve Him in love because we are no longer enemies of God, but His children.

God Gives Us Prayer

Trusting in God to take care of us and our worries, doubts, and fears is a blessing! We don't need to feel like we're giving up control and freedom of our lives. When our capable, loving Father in heaven takes care of us, it's freeing because we don't have that burden to try to carry the "weight of the world" on our shoulders.

We don't have the power and infinite knowledge to be in control of our own lives. God knows all our needs, even before we have needs. But our heavenly Father invites us to do something unique and very special. He asks us to pray to Him, to talk with Him about our anxieties, and to ask Him for anything.

"Do not be anxious about anything, but in everything by prayer and supplication with thanksgiving let your requests be made known to God." (Philippians 4:6)

When we talk with God, it's called prayer. When we share our thoughts with God, it shows that we trust in Him to answer our prayers and to do for us what He knows is best. We share with Him what's important to us and what concerns us. We thank Him for how He's blessed us, and we tell Him how much it means to us that He is all-powerful and all-knowing. We ask Him to provide for our needs and also to provide for the needs of others.

God has promised to hear us!

"Ask, and it will be given to you; seek, and you will find; knock, and it will be opened to you." (Matthew 7:7)

We talk to God, and God talks to us through His Word. When we read the Bible and participate in devotions and Bible study, God will give us the encouragement and comfort that we need to hear, depending on the daily circumstances we're facing. He knows just what we need to hear.

The same is true when we hear God's Word during a worship service. Through the Holy Spirit at work, a pastor will help explain the Scriptures, and it is always just what we need to hear that week. The same Bible story or section of Scripture you've previously read will mean something different to you the next time you read it because you're going through different circumstances in your life.

God's Word can also be shared through other Christians who speak encouragement to you using His Word of comfort. When you speak the Word of God to others in need, the Holy Spirit works through you to build the **Body of Christ**, His Church.

Why do Christians put so much emphasis on prayer and reading the Bible? There is power in God's Word! It is living and active (Hebrews 4:12)! Jesus Christ is the Word (John 1:1). His Word is the way (means) that God shares His grace with us. A special way to pray is to use Bible verses in the wording of our prayers.

What happens when we don't read the Bible? Our heavenly Father desires that we continue to learn about Him and to be strengthened by the power of His Word. But just as children can have an estranged relationship with their earthly father, God's children can put up a wall between themselves and their heavenly Father. God is still there, ready to listen and love, but as sinful children, we sometimes stubbornly refuse to talk to and listen to our heavenly Father. When we stop communicating with Him and stop receiving His gifts, guidance, and gentle care through His Word, the power of sin will have an easier time regaining control of our lives.

But there is never such a time as "too late" in God's eyes. For Christ's sake, God always welcomes us back even when we fail to pray, to hear God's Word, to receive the gifts He gives in the Divine Service. Christians are God's children through Baptism, and we talk to our Father in heaven through prayer. He is our loving Father who wants to bless us with good things and wants us to trust in Him to provide.

God speaks to us through His Word, and we respond in **thanksgiving** and praise, showing honor and glory to Him, making requests for our needs and the needs of others, and confessing our sins and repenting.

When can we pray? We can pray at any time and in any place and for anything. When we pray, we ask God to do what He wants for us, that His will be done. We pray that we receive the things we need to take care of ourselves and our families. We pray for help for others who are hurting or who have hurt us. We pray that God would strengthen our faith to accept whatever happens. We thank Him for who He is and what He has done for us. We thank Him for all He does to preserve us in the one true faith.

God answers our prayer in different ways. He can say yes, and we receive what we ask for. He can say no, and we pray for the strength to be content with what we have. Or God can say, "I have a better idea." This means we may not always get exactly what we want or get it when we want it, but we're open to whatever God has in mind for us.

We pray confidently, knowing our Father in heaven has promised to answer and will give everything we need to support our body and our life. It's okay to be dependent upon God; we can be content that God will provide. "The eyes of all look to You, and You give them their food in due season. You open Your hand; You satisfy the desire of every living thing" (Psalm 145:15–16).

We pray confidently, in Jesus' name. It is because of Jesus' sacrifice on the cross and payment for our sins that we can come to God at all. Because of Jesus' work reconciling us to the Father, we are able to approach Him with our requests. Jesus ascended into heaven and sits at God's right hand, interceding for us. Jesus is a mediator between God and us. Ending prayer "in Jesus' name" shows we pray in faith, confidence, and respect.

The Lord's Prayer

The Introduction

Our Father who art in heaven.

Our Father in heaven.

What does this mean? With these words God tenderly invites us to believe that He is our true Father and that we are His true children, so that with all boldness and confidence we may ask Him as dear children ask their dear father.

The First Petition

Hallowed be Thy name.

Hallowed be Your name.

What does this mean? God's name is certainly holy in itself, but we pray in this petition that it may be kept holy among us also.

How is God's name kept holy? God's name is kept holy when the Word of God is taught in its truth and purity, and we, as the children of God, also lead holy lives according to it. Help us to do this, dear Father in heaven! But anyone who teaches or lives contrary to God's Word profanes the name of God among us. Protect us from this, heavenly Father!

The Second Petition

Thy kingdom come.

Your kingdom come.

What does this mean? The kingdom of God certainly comes by itself without our prayer, but we pray in this petition that it may come to us also.

How does God's kingdom come? God's kingdom comes when our heavenly Father gives us His Holy Spirit, so that by His grace we believe His Holy Word and lead godly lives here in time and there in eternity.

The Third Petition

Thy will be done on earth as it is in heaven.

Your will be done on earth as in heaven.

What does this mean? The good and gracious will of God is done even without our prayer, but we pray in this petition that it may be done among us also.

How is God's will done? God's will is done when He breaks and hinders every evil plan and purpose of the devil, the world, and our sinful nature, which do not want us to hallow God's name or let His kingdom come; and when He strengthens and keeps us firm in His Word and faith until we die.

This is His good and gracious will.

The Fourth Petition

Give us this day our daily bread.

Give us today our daily bread.

What does this mean? God certainly gives daily bread to everyone without our prayers, even to all evil people, but we pray in this petition that God would lead us to realize this and to receive our daily bread with thanksgiving.

What is meant by daily bread? Daily bread includes everything that has to do with the support and needs of the body, such as food, drink, clothing, shoes, house, home, land, animals, money, goods, a devout husband or wife, devout children, devout workers, devout and faithful rulers, good government, good weather, peace, health, self-control, good reputation, good friends, faithful neighbors, and the like.

The Fifth Petition

And forgive us our trespasses as we forgive those who trespass against us.

Forgive us our sins as we forgive those who sin against us.

What does this mean? We pray in this petition that our Father in heaven would not look at our sins, or deny our prayer because of them. We are neither worthy of the things for which we pray, nor have we deserved them, but we ask that He would give them all to us by grace, for we daily sin much and surely deserve nothing but punishment. So we too will sincerely forgive and gladly do good to those who sin against us.

The Sixth Petition

And lead us not into temptation.

Lead us not into temptation.

What does this mean? God tempts no one. We pray in this petition that God would guard and keep us so that the devil, the world, and our sinful nature may not deceive us or mislead us into false belief, despair, and other great shame and vice. Although we are attacked by these things, we pray that we may finally overcome them and win the victory.

The Seventh Petition

But deliver us from evil.

But deliver us from evil.

What does this mean? We pray in this petition, in summary, that our Father in heaven would rescue us from every evil of body and soul, possessions and reputation, and finally, when our last hour comes, give us a blessed end, and graciously take us from this valley of sorrow to Himself in heaven.

The Conclusion

For Thine is the kingdom and the power and the glory forever and ever.* Amen.

For the kingdom, the power, and the glory are Yours now and forever. Amen.*

What does this mean? This means that I should be certain that these petitions are pleasing to our Father in heaven, and are heard by Him; for He Himself has commanded us to pray in this way and has promised to hear us. Amen, amen means "yes, yes, it shall be so."

* These words were not in Luther's Small Catechism.

Praying His Prayer

Jesus taught us a prayer that captures all that we should include in a prayer.

Heavenly Father

When we pray the Lord's Prayer, we confess our trust in our heavenly Father to be in control and to provide for all our needs—spiritually and physically.

His Kingdom

Christians are members of God's kingdom of grace, the Church on earth. We want to live godly lives as members of His Church. And we pray that all people would be a part of the Church to receive His blessings! When we pray about eternity, we're wanting God's kingdom of glory (the Church and angels in heaven) to come soon. Jesus will come again.

God's Will

We pray not only for our own wants, but also for what is best for God's kingdom. When we pray the Lord's Prayer, we are in step with the First Commandment as we fear, love, and trust in God above all things. Jesus prayed that if it was God's will, the cup of suffering would be lifted from Him. But God knew it was best for the whole world if Jesus suffered and died so the promise of salvation would be fulfilled.

Forgiving Trespasses

Trespass is a word for sin that means "to step over the line." Our sins make us worthy of nothing but punishment. It is only because of Jesus' forgiveness that we can confidently come to God in prayer. When we forgive those who have wronged us—even though it's difficult—we are showing we truly believe that God has had mercy on us.

Encountering Temptation

We pray that God would give us strength to resist the attempts of the devil, our culture, and our own sinful self to get us to do things that are against God, which is the opposite of what is best for us. We ask God to give us strength to overcome the temptations of our spiritual enemies that lure us away from God and His ways.

Deliverance from Evil

God might test our faith and we might encounter suffering, but the purpose is that we would draw near to God and realize our dependence on Him. It is for our good, to produce character and hope. God uses suffering to bring us to a closer relationship with Him, but we pray that He would keep us from harm. When we do encounter troubles, we pray that He would give us the strength to get through them. We look forward to the time when we will no longer experience sadness and pain.

Living as God's Child

This chapter looks at the life of a Christian as a baptized child of God. Baptism, a gift of God, is a Sacrament in which God unites water and His Word to give forgiveness and countless other blessings. After exploring our new identity in Christ through Baptism, we also address in this chapter how God takes care of us and invites us to talk with Him on a daily basis through prayer.

God Gives Us New Life

One of the amazing aspects of Baptism is that it gives us new life. Jesus was baptized, died, and rose. When we are baptized, our sinful selves die and we receive new life now and the promise of eternal life when we die. This is an amazing mystery and a sure promise of God.

Review Romans 6:3–5. Read it slowly, taking in the amazing power of Baptism.

God Gives Us a Name

What's in a name? In Baptism, God calls us by name. And He commands us to use His triune name when baptizing. Those who are baptized are marked with God's own name and are adopted as His children. With this new name, we have a new identity in Christ.

Review Matthew 28:19. The name of our triune God is not merely a set of "magic words." It is an essential piece of the Sacrament of Holy Baptism, which unites God's Word and promise to simple water for forgiveness of sins. This is much more than any magic trick.

God Gives Us What We Need

As God's beloved children, we can trust that our heavenly Father will give us everything we need. Much like earthly parents, He does not give us everything we want. But He always does what is best for us.

Review 1 Corinthians 4:7. Our society chafes at words that contradict our illusion of independence. But Christians know that God is the source of every good thing.

God Gives Us Peace

It can be confusing for new Christians to see that things are still difficult here on earth. Yes, God is in control. But this fallen world still suffers from the consequences of sin. Believers cast their cares on the Lord and trust that He will work even tragedy for good (Romans 8:28).

Review Matthew 6:25, 27. Think about the fruitlessness of worry and anxiety when we have a loving, powerful God.

God Gives Us Free Will

God chose us before creation to be His people. He comes to us with His Word and through His Holy Spirit to create faith in us. He promises that nothing can separate us from His love—even Satan himself. Why, then, don't all people believe? We are not robots, forced to love God. Some people reject God and His love.

Review John 10:28. Consider the comfort this gives even during the most difficult times in life.

God Gives Us Prayer

We are given access to the almighty God of the universe! God invites us to pray to Him as children approach their father. We talk to our heavenly Father, and He responds through His Word. He promises to answer our prayers in the way that is best for us.

Review Psalm 145:15–16. God cares for every living thing. That's a promise.

Living as God's Child

This page serves two purposes. First, it provides questions for you to consider. But it also provides a blank section to store your own questions.

If you're using this book for personal study, this is a great way to record any questions you still have. Then find a time to meet with a pastor, church leader, or church friend to talk things through. **If you meet with a class**, your questions can help fuel great discussion during class time.

Warning: You might need extra writing space.

God Gives Us New Life

- Who needs Baptism?
- List at least three benefits God gives in Baptism.

God Gives Us a Name

- We are baptized in the name of ___________ . Why is this name so important?

God Gives Us What We Need

- Do children always get what they want? What about the children of God?
- Explain the importance of a loving and powerful God who knows what we need.

God Gives Us Peace

- When things seem beyond hope, where can we find peace? Record a comforting Bible passage here, and share it with others.

God Gives Us Free Will

- If someone believes in God, who gets the credit? If someone rejects God, who gets the "credit"?

God Gives Us Prayer

- Consider your prayer life right now. What would you like to adapt for your prayer routine?
- Consider your most common prayers. Are there topics you dwell on? Are there topics you omit?

Your Questions

Try a journal or some large adhesive notes.

TIP

CHAPTER 4

Living the Christian Life

We were created to do good works (Ephesians 2:10)! By the power of the Holy Spirit's life-giving work and in thanksgiving to God, our actions, thoughts, and words are guided by the Ten Commandments. They describe more than just the things we avoid doing. They teach us the wonderful ways in which we show love to God and to others, our families, friends, co-workers, even our enemies. By our actions and words, we live to give glory and honor to God, not ourselves. Bottom line: we live to serve others.

The Bible often describes good works as "bearing fruit." This is a wonderful way to think about the good works we do for others. The branches of a fruit tree bear fruit, not the roots or the trunk. But if the roots or the trunk are not healthy, the branches cannot bear fruit. In Baptism, we are grafted into Christ. We were once branches bearing bad fruit because of sin. When we are grafted into Christ, we are connected to the good, healthy root system and strong trunk. Only because of Christ, and through Christ, can we be branches that bear fruit, or good works. Those around us benefit from these good works, and we benefit from the good works that others do.

The Holy Spirit makes us holy. The work of the Holy Spirit is called **sanctification**. The Holy Spirit is our helper, enabling us to live as God's children. He gives us faith in the Savior. Our response to the Good News about Jesus saving us is thanksgiving and a new attitude to live a Christian life, obeying God, resisting temptation and sin, and bearing fruit in good works and love for our neighbors.

God Gives Us Purpose

As we strive each day to trust in God's care for us and to leave things in His hands, we rely on the Holy Spirit's power. God commands us to have no other gods; He alone is God. Through the Holy Spirit, we are given the ability to fear, love, and trust in Him more than anything else.

© iStock / Pamela Moore

The Holy Spirit makes us new each day. Through Baptism, we are new creations. Through daily remembrance of our Baptism, our sinful nature is drowned and dies. The Bible calls those sinful tendencies works of **the flesh**: "sexual immorality, impurity, sensuality, idolatry, sorcery, enmity, strife, jealousy, fits of anger, rivalries, dissensions, divisions, envy, drunkenness, orgies, and things like these" (Galatians 5:19–21).

In its place, the Spirit gives new life—a resurrection—and fills us with **"love, joy, peace, patience, kindness, goodness, faithfulness, gentleness, [and] self-control" (Galatians 5:22-23)**. There is no law against those things. If the Spirit lives in us, working through our hands, mouths, minds, and bodies, we no longer need to fear the Law (Galatians 5:18).

The Holy Spirit exchanges our sinful nature for a godly, spiritual nature. The Holy Spirit replaces the lies of sin with the truth of God. In the truth and purity of God, we no longer serve the creature (ourselves). We serve the Creator (Romans 1:24–26).

Freedom in Christ

Christians do not need to live each day wracked with fear and guilt. We have been set free from the guilt of sin. Each day (each moment!), we remember the Gospel message: in Christ, we are forgiven! Sin no longer has power over us. We are not controlled by our sinful flesh. We also don't need to be haunted by sins of the past. Jesus has forgiven those sins already! Consequences may linger, but God's forgiveness of our sins for Jesus' sake always remains.

After the Holy Spirit creates faith through God's Word and Baptism, the Law still has meaning for us, every day. Because we still sin and are tempted to sin, the Law reminds us of our sin, convicting us as sinners. Through faith in Jesus, we repent and run back to the cross of Christ for His constant forgiveness.

"For freedom Christ has set us free." (Galatians 5:1)

Jesus has freed us from the power of sin, death, and the devil. We are free to serve God. We're not restrained or constrained anymore; we desire to please God, and we can, do, and will please God by our Spirit-sanctified thoughts, words, and actions that show love to others (Galatians 5:13).

God Gives Us Freedom

Some people think Christians are moralistic and rigid. It's important to realize that we don't do good works and try to "be good" in order to win God's favor. Through Jesus, we already have been reconciled to God. We do good works, serving our neighbors, because we want to give glory to God and to thank Him for His blessings. "We love because He first loved us" (1 John 4:19). When we fail and sin, we're not devastated because of God's wrath; we simply repent and turn back to His Law as a guide for our daily living. "Beloved, let us love one another, for love is from God. . . . God sent His only Son into the world, so that we might live through Him. In this is love, not that we have loved God but that He loved us and sent His Son. . . . Beloved, if God so loved us, we also ought to love one another" (1 John 4:7, 9–11).

Some Christians *do* focus on the Law too much; this is called legalism. Some people think that Jesus saved us by taking care of the big sins, or our sinful nature, but that their own good works *sustain* their salvation—that by being good enough, they won't lose their "ticket" to heaven.

These ideas are not true. Jesus saved us completely on the cross by His suffering and death. Not only for us, but for all people of all times. Through faith in Jesus, the Holy Spirit truly made us **saints** of God, pure and holy in His eyes. Each day, we focus on what God has done for us in Christ and then live through the Holy Spirit at work in us through the Word and Sacraments.

Our freedom is found in throwing off our desire to sin or the temptation to be drawn back into guilt for past sins. Our freedom is to enjoy loving others. There is great satisfaction and joy found in serving others in love without obligation. Our freedom is found in enjoying God's blessings of food and drink, hard work and relaxation, worship and His divine gifts, and family and friends who love us and bring us laughter and joy.

What is a saint?

We often think of saints as special people who have died, who never really sinned, or who did super good works in their lifetime. However, *all* Christians are actually saints! Saints *are* holy and perfect people . . . because Jesus has made them so by washing their sins away. We may not feel like we're doing amazing things, but God is at work through us. We also don't have to wait until we have died in order to be "sainted."

Why do people think Christians don't "walk the walk"? Lutherans have a special way of describing ourselves. We say we are both saint and sinner at the same time. We are made into a new, holy (righteous) self in Baptism. Our new self is the new spiritual life and nature, created in us by the washing of rebirth (Titus 3:5).

But in this earthly life, where the consequences of sin remain, our old, sinful nature inside will continually attempt to control our actions and desires. Every day is a battle between the saint and sinner within ourselves. Through our Baptism, our new self overcomes sin. Each day, we can live a new life in Christ and grow before God in faith and good works.

Jesus has saved all of us, once and for all (Hebrews 10:10). All in Him are saints. But being a Christian doesn't just mean we've been converted and have faith and that's all there is to it. Sanctification is the spiritual growth that follows justification. *Each day* and *each moment,* we need God's Word so that we are always repenting and experiencing Christ's forgiveness. Our response to the Gospel is faith, and the Christian life is all about growing in faith. Although we are forgiven, we continue to sin. It may be confusing to non-Christians. But Christians cling to the sure hope that *in heaven* our sanctification will be complete (1 Corinthians 15:49).

A Clean Heart

The Holy Spirit not only calls you by the Gospel and gives you saving faith, but throughout your earthly life, the Holy Spirit also daily renews and cleanses you so that you strive to overcome evil desires and do good works as you live in Him. Through the Word and Sacraments, your trust in God will be strengthened. Each day, you can pray,

"Create in me a clean heart, O God, and renew a right spirit within me" (Psalm 51:10).

The drowning of our sinful nature through Baptism is something that happens each day. Yes, it is a struggle to resist sin and temptation, but the Holy Spirit is our helper. He changes us; He increases our knowledge of God and gives us the desire to live according to His Law. Remember: the Ten Commandments are the ways God describes how His people live. The Holy Spirit does all this through the powerful Word of God.

When we wrestle with our sinful nature and recognize that our thoughts and behaviors don't align with God's Ten Commandments, we feel sorry. When we recognize our sin and turn in faith to God for His mercy, it's called repentance. Through God's Word, the Holy Spirit changes our hearts so that we desire to live life according to God's Word (instead of living life according to our own human desires). Living according to God's Word produces good works, which are the fruits of repentance (Matthew 3:8). The Holy Spirit's work of making you holy (sanctification) is transformative work (Romans 12:2), and it is daily work. "For to set the mind on the flesh is death, but to set the mind on the Spirit is life and peace. . . . You, however, are not in the flesh but in the Spirit, if in fact the Spirit of God dwells in you" (Romans 8:6, 9).

What is a disciple?

Disciples are followers who have learned to believe in the lessons of their teacher. Jesus' whole life was a model of what love looks like. As the twelve disciples served as apprentices under Jesus, we see Jesus in His Word. God, who has given us the Scriptures to make us "wise for salvation" (2 Timothy 3:15), opens our eyes to believe in Jesus, our Savior who humbly serves His people (Mark 9:35).

The same Holy Spirit who *brought us to faith* continues to work in us *to keep us steadfast and grow in faith* through God's Word and the Sacraments, making us His disciples, individuals whom He has called and equipped to serve the Lord and others. Discipleship is more than knowing Jesus and listening to His Word; it also involves an application to our lives and a commitment to follow and to serve.

Dig a Little Deeper

READ John 13:12–17 to see how Jesus leads His disciples by example in serving others.

READ Luke 5:1–11, where Jesus calls His disciples to catch others by witnessing to God's Word.

If you're a fan of a sports team, others around you most likely know it. You may go to games, watch on your TV or device, talk about the team, and wear clothing that shows your support of the team.

Our Christian words and actions toward others work the same way. Others will see that we belong to God by our going to church, studying the Bible at home and with other Christians, and making choices that reflect God's will for us. The way we dress, speak, and live point to the team we belong to—the family of God.

Confession

What is Confession?

Confession has two parts.

First, that we confess our sins, and second, that we receive absolution, that is, forgiveness, from the pastor as from God Himself, not doubting, but firmly believing that by it our sins are forgiven before God in heaven.

What sins should we confess?

Before God we should plead guilty of all sins, even those we are not aware of, as we do in the Lord's Prayer; but before the pastor we should confess only those sins which we know and feel in our hearts.

Which are these?

Consider your place in life according to the Ten Commandments: Are you a father, mother, son, daughter, husband, wife, or worker? Have you been disobedient, unfaithful, or lazy? Have you been hot-tempered, rude, or quarrelsome? Have you hurt someone by your words or deeds? Have you stolen, been negligent, wasted anything, or done any harm?

The Bible says, **"We . . . are being transformed"** (2 Corinthians 3:18).

Repentance and renewal are daily deeds done by the Holy Spirit until the day we die.

What is the Office of the Keys?

The Office of the Keys is that special authority which Christ has given to His church on earth to forgive the sins of repentant sinners, but to withhold forgiveness from the unrepentant as long as they do not repent.

Where is this written?

This is what St. John the Evangelist writes in chapter twenty: The Lord Jesus breathed on His disciples and said, "Receive the Holy Spirit. If you forgive anyone his sins, they are forgiven; if you do not forgive them, they are not forgiven." (John 20:22–23)

What do you believe according to these words?

I believe that when the called ministers of Christ deal with us by His divine command, in particular when they exclude openly unrepentant sinners from the Christian congregation and absolve those who repent of their sins and want to do better, this is just as valid and certain, even in heaven, as if Christ our dear Lord dealt with us Himself.

God Gives Us Forgiveness

Repentance is not just devout-sounding-yet-empty moaning about how we are rotten sinners. Repentance is "to turn," to leave behind the sin we love so much. We are unable to repent without the Holy Spirit. Repentance is a gift from God, bestowed by the Holy Spirit. *He* changes our attitudes. When we delight in sinful behaviors, He convicts us with the Law. When we think about the sinful things we want to do, He knows that too and uses our conscience to convict us. Repentance is never fun, never pretty, but it always has a purpose. Through repentance, the Holy Spirit always leads us to Christ.

When we say we're sorry for our sins, either publicly (in church, with the rest of the **congregation**) or privately (with a pastor), it's called confession. We're admitting what we've done wrong. This takes self-reflection and honesty. We're good at making excuses for the sinful things we do. We all know how to sugarcoat the truth about our sin, comparing it to the much worse sin we see in others or fooling ourselves into thinking that nobody knows about *that* sin anyway. But God does. "If we say we have no sin, we deceive ourselves, and the truth is not in us. If we confess our sins, He is faithful and just to forgive us our sins and to cleanse us from all unrighteousness" (1 John 1:8–9).

The point of confession isn't that the pastor wants to know how bad you've been. The point is that our pastors want us to know the freedom of forgiveness. The weight of our sin and shame has been lifted! Jesus paid for all our sins, even the ones we don't admit, even the ones we don't recognize as sins. Pastors want us to have the peace of Christ that can be found only when we are truly guilt-free. "Repent therefore, and turn back [to God], that your sins may be blotted out, that times of refreshing may come from the presence of the Lord" (Acts 3:19–20).

Confession is always immediately followed by God's forgiveness. God works through the pastor to speak His words of comfort to us. The **Office of the Keys** means that the Bible promises that when the pastor declares us forgiven for the sake of Christ, it is as if we hear it from the mouth of God Himself. God is speaking through our pastors. The door to God's heavenly kingdom has been opened to us through Christ.

God removes the burden of sin that controls our actions and removes the weight of guilt and regret. True peace is knowing that through Jesus, everything is right between you and God. "As far as the east is from the west, so far does He remove our transgressions from us" (Psalm 103:12).

Children of Light

The Bible describes the work of the Holy Spirit as choosing us and calling us out of darkness into His marvelous light (1 Peter 2:9). He "enlightens" us by His gifts. Jesus gave "light to those who sit in darkness and in the shadow of death, to guide our feet into the way of peace" (Luke 1:79). He is the light of the world. Without the light, we don't know which way to go in this life, and we certainly don't know the way to get to eternal life. The Holy Spirit gives us faith in our Savior, which saves us.

We are "children of light," and we discern what is pleasing to the Lord through His Word and by letting the Holy Spirit do His work through us. Paul encourages us to "shine as lights in the world" (Philippians 2:15) to a twisted generation. **"It is God who works in you, both to will and to work for His good pleasure" (Philippians 2:13)**. No matter the task, we humbly live for God and bring glory to Him! "Let us cast off the works of darkness and put on the armor of light" (Romans 13:12).

Holy Communion

What is the Sacrament of the Altar?

It is the true body and blood of our Lord Jesus Christ under the bread and wine, instituted by Christ Himself for us Christians to eat and to drink.

Where is this written?

The holy Evangelists Matthew, Mark, Luke, and St. Paul write:

Our Lord Jesus Christ, on the night when He was betrayed, took bread, and when He had given thanks, He broke it and gave it to the disciples and said: "Take eat; this is My body, which is given for you. This do in remembrance of Me."

In the same way also He took the cup after supper, and when He had given thanks, He gave it to them, saying, "Drink of it, all of you; this cup is the new testament in My blood, which is shed for you for the forgiveness of sins. This do, as often as you drink it, in remembrance of Me."

What is the benefit of this eating and drinking?

These words, "Given and shed for you for the forgiveness of sins," show us that in the Sacrament forgiveness of sins, life, and salvation are given us through these words. For where there is forgiveness of sins, there is also life and salvation.

How can bodily eating and drinking do such great things?

Certainly not just eating and drinking do these things, but the words written here: "Given and shed for you for the forgiveness of sins." These words, along with the bodily eating and drinking, are the main thing in the Sacrament. Whoever believes these words has exactly what they say: "forgiveness of sins."

Who receives this sacrament worthily?

Fasting and bodily preparation are certainly fine outward training. But that person is truly worthy and well prepared who has faith in these words: "Given and shed for you for the forgiveness of sins."

But anyone who does not believe these words or doubts them is unworthy and unprepared, for the words "for you" require all hearts to believe.

Forgiving Others

In the Lord's Prayer, we pray "forgive us our trespasses as we forgive those who trespass against us." Even though sin still clings to us, Jesus told us we can pray to our heavenly Father to forgive us for Christ's sake. The God who created us and condemned us for our sins is now *our Father* to whom we pray. As a sign of God's great forgiveness to us, *we* forgive *others* their sins.

We forgive even if we've been mistreated. We forgive even if we feel we're entitled to some kind of restitution or compensation for being wronged. But if we do *not* forgive others, we hold on to unneeded bitterness and anger. It hurts us not only emotionally and spiritually, but physically as well.

"If you do not forgive others their trespasses, neither will your Father forgive your trespasses" (Matthew 6:15). When we find it difficult to forgive others, God makes it possible. He reminds us through Word and Sacrament that the Holy Spirit gives us the power to forgive others, even if they don't deserve it. Only through the Holy Spirit's work in our hearts can we be moved to show mercy. To forgive is to love. God shows us this love, and we show it to others (1 John 4:7–21).

Thankfully, God doesn't keep score with us. We'd never meet His expectations. Daily, He forgives us. Christian families don't keep score with one another either. Daily, we forgive one another. Christian spouses and children regularly won't live up to our expectations. Once forgiven by God through His Word and Sacraments, we are free to love and serve others. This is especially true for those "neighbors" closest to you—the ones inside your home.

When you have an attitude of joyfully serving the other members of your family, you won't be bitter if you've changed more diapers, washed more dishes or loads of laundry, or picked up more things off the floor than other family members. The Holy Spirit makes the words of our mouths and the meditation of our hearts pleasing in God's sight (Psalm 19:14). Knowing we are forgiven, we can find that extra measure of patience or joy in our family service. Knowing the Holy Spirit is able to replace our grumbling words with contentment and a new song (Psalm 40:3), we recognize the joy in loving. We don't need high praise or appreciation in return! If it comes, we rejoice. If it does not, we carry on loving "because He first loved us" (1 John 4:19)

Just as family members can fight, brothers and sisters in Christ can fight and be less than the perfect and holy family that God expects them to be. Those who are outside of the family of God may not understand how we can be saints (holy) and sinners at the same time. But the Church is for sinful and broken people. It's a place where we practice forgiveness and reconciliation. We don't get it right every time. Things may go wrong—very wrong—but in the family of God, Jesus makes things right and the Holy Spirit gives us second chances by daily renewing us.

In a healthy family, there is a sense of security in knowing that even if things go wrong, there is still a family bond. In the Church, this bond is actually more profound. Through Baptism, we become a part of the Body of Christ, not bodies, not organizations or **denominations**, but the one, unified Body of Christ.

The Christian life is a daily battle. Thankfully, God sustains and strengthens our faith. God creates in us a new heart that *enjoys and wants to* live according to His ways. God works sanctification only through the Means of Grace. The second sacrament in which God gives grace is the Lord's Supper. Through the Lord's Supper, we receive forgiveness of sins. Christ tells us to regularly eat and drink at His Holy Table, receiving His body and blood with the bread and wine.

The Lord's Supper is a sacrament because it was instituted (initiated and commanded) by our Lord. He said "do this" in remembrance of Him. But it is not a mere meal in which we remember who Jesus is and what He did. Here, Jesus gives us a new sacrament, using basic physical things (bread and wine) that are connected to His powerful Word so that we may receive a tremendous blessing. Jesus said, "This is My body. . . . This is My blood," and it was given to us "for the forgiveness of sins" (Matthew 26:26, 28). We need the forgiveness of sins and the strength for a new and holy life.

Through this means, we are connected to Christ. Jesus is present in His meal! He is with us, supplying our spiritual needs. Jesus said, "I am the vine; you are the branches. Whoever abides in Me and I in him, he it is that bears much fruit, for apart from Me you can do nothing" (John 15:5).

Grafting a branch (sinner) to a healthy root (Jesus) requires cutting (the Law/Word of God), but the result is that the new branch (saint) is connected to a healthy root (Jesus/the Gospel/Word of God). Through this healthy root, the branch grows, is strengthened, and bears fruit (good works for others).

In our Baptism, we are cut off from our old "root" (our own human desires). Jesus is our new rootstock, supplying what we need to be spiritually healthy and strong through Word and Sacrament and granting us the Holy Spirit to help us bear fruit (loving our neighbors). His blood, like the sap in a tree, is the constant, life-giving source for the repentant believer!

God Gives Us the Church

The Church is one Body, with Christ as the Head (Colossians 1:18). Through the Holy Spirit, the Body of Christ (the Church) practices unconditional love, each member working together. We are different members, or parts, that together make one whole Body, each part vitally important.

We all have different things we're good at and different ways to serve one another. The Holy Spirit has blessed us each individually with gifts in order to serve.

The Church is also described as a family. We are brothers and sisters in Christ. There is only one universal (**catholic**) Church, made up of all believers in Christ. This is called the invisible Church. We have a special connection.

"There is one body and one Spirit . . . one Lord, one faith, one baptism, one God and Father of all, who is over all and through all and in all." (Ephesians 4:4-6)

But there are many different denominations, which are church organizations with a distinct name and set of beliefs. Wherever Christians physically gather for worship, prayer and praise to God, and to receive His gifts—within homes or denominational buildings or sanctuaries (e.g., Lutheran, Baptist, Roman Catholic, Presbyterian, etc.)—here we *see* the visible Church. We pray that our Lutheran denomination rightly teaches the Word of God and shares the Sacraments according to God's command. Not all who claim to be Christian are Christian. The Bible gives many warnings of avoiding false teachers and false **doctrine**.

The Church is also called the communion of saints. Through Christ, all believers are joined together through faith given by the Holy Spirit. The Holy Spirit continues to grow the Church by adding more people by calling them to saving faith in Christ. The Holy Spirit also preserves the Church by keeping the Church strong in faith toward Christ and in love toward one another.

We are called Christians because we are believers in Christ, but also because the Church is built on *Christ* alone. Jesus is the firm foundation of the Church, upon which everything else stands (1 Corinthians 3:11).

It is through Christ alone that we are saved. It is through Christ alone that we are reconciled to God the Father and that we have a restored relationship with Him. It is through Christ alone that we have eternal life. Any other belief about true peace and fullness of life is like sinking, shifting sand. Only the Word of God is the solid, unmoving rock. Jesus said He would build His Church on the rock-solid truth that He is the Christ, the Son of the living God (Matthew 16:15).

Basic Bible Teachings

Holy Communion

The Lord's Supper is also called Holy Communion. When you are "in communion" with someone, you have a close relationship to that person. It is an intimate, close fellowship and time of sharing. God created us to be "in communion" with Him. Sin destroyed that communion.

- Through faith, we have communion with Jesus. He is present with us. We come to the Lord's Table empty, worn, and weak. Jesus fills us up to overflowing with Himself to strengthen and preserve us! We need that forgiveness and strength for a new and holy life, and we need it often.
- Jesus said, "This is My body. . . . This is My blood" (Matthew 26:26, 28). Lutherans believe what Jesus said! He is truly present in the meal. It is the true body and blood of Jesus under the bread and wine. "The cup of blessing that we bless, is it not a participation in the blood of Christ? The bread that we break, is it not a participation in the body of Christ?" (1 Corinthians 10:16). The bread and wine remain, but through the power of God's Word, Christ gives us His body and blood in, with, and under the blessed (consecrated) bread and wine. This is called the **real presence**.
- The Lord's Supper is Jesus' last will and **testament**. When He first instituted His Supper, He gave the entire Church the inheritance He won for us on the cross at His death. A last will and testament can only be given when the benefactor dies. Jesus alone is that benefactor and so commanded that after His death we remember Him and continue to distribute His body and blood, which bring the gift of forgiveness of sins, life, and salvation. This is His **covenant**—His promise. And nothing will break His promise; we will be with Him forever.
- We have communion with other believers, even the saints (believers) who are in heaven. In a Divine Worship service, a hymn of praise is often sung before the Sacrament of the Altar. Many times, Scripture tells us that the angels around God's throne in heaven sing "holy, holy, holy." We join the angels at this time, singing praise to the Holy, Holy, Holy Lord God of Israel. On the altar rests the body and blood of Christ, soon to be on our lips. The communion between God and mankind is restored through Jesus, and all of the company of heaven rejoices with us.
- **"Because there is one bread, we who are many are one body, for we all partake of the one bread" (1 Corinthians 10:17).** We share fellowship with all the believers communing with us. We all confess the same thing regarding what we believe about the Meal. We all believe that Jesus died for us to forgive our sins and rose again to give us eternal life. We are one in Christ (Galatians 3:28).

God Gives Us Worship

We are sinful people, but in His mercy, Holy God comes to us. In corporate worship, when God's people join together, we gather in the Lord's house, His **sanctuary**, where He is present and we receive God's gifts. It is His *divine service* to us.

We begin in our triune God's name (the Invocation). God has promised that where His name is, He is there. Right away, we confess our sins and receive God's forgiveness (Confession and **Absolution**). Because Jesus took the punishment we deserved, our sins are gone and we are able to stand in the presence of a holy, perfect God.

Because of Jesus, when we're in God's presence we don't fear Him. We remember that He remains our all-powerful, all-knowing God, and we show proper respect and reverence in this special gathering place. But when we come to Divine Service, we need not worry about being punished. We come to worship because here God invites us to come. Here, we see the magnitude of His love as He gives us His gifts and shows us His love. The means, or way, through which He does this is His Word and Sacraments.

Often, we humbly kneel during Confession or kneel at the Communion rail when we reach the Lord's Table. But God doesn't knock us down or punish us as we deserve. It's here that God lifts up humble people (Psalm 147:6). He restores our soul (Psalm 23:3) and renews our spirit. We come to God empty, but He fills us with His power and His peace.

Divine Service

Corporate worship is the gathering of Christians to respond to God's mercy and grace with thanksgiving, prayer, and praise. The Divine Service is the service to which God calls and gathers His people to give to them the gifts of life and salvation by means of Word and Sacrament.

In the Lutheran Church, we refer to our times of corporate worship as Divine Service. *Divine* means it is all about God; it is Christ-centered. *Service* means that God comes to serve us with His gifts. The order of the worship service has been developed among Christians all around the world from the very beginning of the time of the New Testament. It is based entirely on God's Word and is completely focused on what Jesus has done for us to reconcile us to God.

In Divine Service, God gives us His gifts of forgiveness of sins, life, and salvation. His Word comforts us, strengthens us, and renews us. God comes to us in the Bible readings, the preaching that explains God's Word, the **liturgy** (order of service) that is made up of God's Word, the music that includes and expounds God's Word, Holy Baptism, and Holy Communion. In response, we worship and adore the one true God with prayer, hymns of thanksgiving, and hymns of praise.

Life of Praise

So if worship is really all about what God does for us, then what do we do? The Holy Spirit calls, gathers, and

enlightens us. By faith, we realize that we need God. We thank Him for His gifts to us! We respond with a grateful heart. We recognize God's power and mercy, and we praise Him. We all need God's mercy; we corporately pray for others in need of God's healing and compassion.

When you treasure time to worship God, the blessings from this time flow into the rest of your week. We don't stop giving God thanks and praise just because Monday morning hits again. And God certainly is faithful, giving us life and forgiveness each day. Each morning, God's mercies are new (Lamentations 3:22–23). Each morning, we remember our Baptism and the promise that today God re-creates us in Christ for love and service.

- We daily respond in gratitude.
- We give God honor through our God-pleasing words and actions.
- We give God glory by sharing His gifts and serving others.

On Sunday mornings, through Confession and Absolution, the proclamation of God's Word, and Holy Communion, we are forgiven and strengthened by God. Throughout the week, God uses *us* to dispense and disperse His gifts (forgiveness and mercy) to *others* as we serve them. This brings glory to God because it points to Him, the giver of life and every blessing.

God shows us His great love for us, and we respond. God invites us to be with Him, and so we nurture our relationship with Him by spending time with Him at His house (of worship) and in His Word (at worship and throughout the week through Bible reading and prayer).

The Church in Action

Since we are the Church, we serve. Through us, God takes care of the needs of others. We give our time, our talents, and our financial resources to serve others. Everything we have is a gift from God; we pray that the Holy Spirit would guide us in using those gifts wisely to take care of all whom God places before us with a need.

We give because we have received Christ's love. Our motivation isn't guilt, but freedom to share what we have, trusting in God to provide for our needs. Our motivation isn't obligation, but gratitude.

Jesus Himself descended from His heavenly throne and humbly took on our flesh, coming to earth as a servant, to live and die among sinners. He served sinners. He always put the needs of others first. He counsels us, "Whoever would be great among you must be your servant, and whoever would be first among you must be your slave" (Matthew 20:26–27).

"But you are a chosen race, a royal priesthood, a holy nation, a people for His own possession, that you may proclaim the excellencies of Him who called you out of darkness into His marvelous light" (1 Peter 2:9). Being a member of the priesthood of believers means that in our daily lives, we can "proclaim the excellencies" of our Savior. As members of the priesthood, we also work in our daily lives to share praise of Jesus with others.

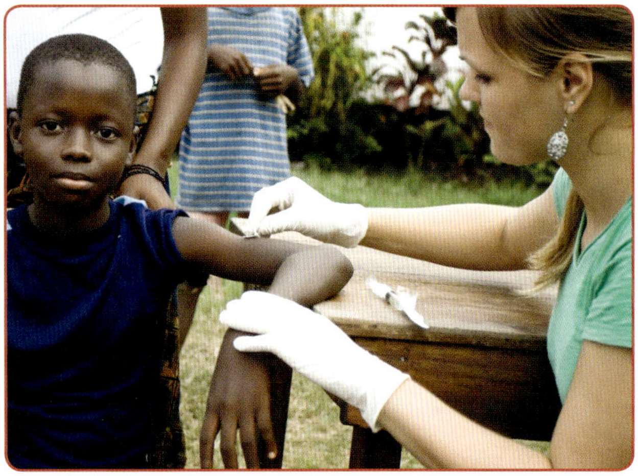

God Gives Us a Commission

The Church Witnesses

Like we read in the Book of Acts and in Paul's letters, God delivers His Word, and the Good News of our salvation, through men and women who make up His Church. Our merciful God knows that our world is hurting and that all people need to know the hope and life we have in Christ. This is the Church's **mission**.

Jesus prays in the Lord's Prayer "Thy kingdom come." We pray that everyone would know of God's love, believe in Him, be joined to the Body of Christ in His kingdom of grace. We pray that everyone would be able to live with the saints and angels in His heavenly kingdom of glory forever.

God saved everyone everywhere through Christ, but not everyone everywhere knows what Jesus has done. Before returning to His heavenly kingdom, Jesus gave a special responsibility to His Church through His disciples. We call this the Great Commission, and it is the fulfillment of this commission that spreads the Word of God so that others indeed might hear and believe. Jesus said:

"Go therefore and make disciples of all nations, baptizing them in the name of the Father and of the Son and of the Holy Spirit, teaching them to observe all that I have commanded you" (Matthew 28:19-20).

The Church Prays

As brothers and sisters in Christ, we care about one another and pray together as a congregation for one another's needs. God speaks to us through His Word, so we listen to His words of encouragement and guidance and speak our concerns to God. You may think that others make empty promises when they say "I'm praying for you" or "You're in my thoughts and prayers." But such promises are not empty. Such conversations take place in the presence of the Holy Spirit. Such conversations make our needs known to the Lord, and the Holy Spirit speaks directly to the Father on our behalf (Romans 8:26–27). In all things, we commend our prayer requests to God because we know He's the one who has the authority to do something about them.

We often include petitions in our prayers

- for the local congregation and the Church at large;
- for right teaching;
- for protection from the assaults of the devil;
- for the government;
- for those who suffer;
- for the welfare and safety of ourselves and others;
- for the conversion of the unbeliever; and
- for the restoration of those who have left the Church.

The Church Serves

Every Christian is called by God into various **vocations**. Child, parent, friend, teacher, accountant, politician, cook—all of these are vocations. Church member, family member, community member—all of these are vocations too. A vocation is simply a role we are given by God; through this role, we serve others in Christian love. There is more to our vocations than what we can see. God works through our particular roles and tasks to take care of His creation. God works through us to show His love and mercy to others. When we serve others in our vocations—our daily routines and ordinary relationships—we love God and we love one another (Matthew 22:36–40).

Vocations are "masks of God." Behind the face of a father, teacher, store clerk, nurse, or police officer, God is there, ministering to us through them. We are the hands and feet of Jesus as God works through us in our ordinary circumstances.

"Whatever you do, in word or deed, do everything in the name of the Lord Jesus, giving thanks to God the Father through Him." (Colossians 3:17)

The Church Waits

Like a bride waits with great anticipation for her wedding day, so we, the Church, wait for the return of Jesus, our Bridegroom. In the Book of Revelation, the Church is called the **Bride of Christ**. This language may seem strange. But the Church views this metaphor as a beautiful picture of Jesus' unconditional love for us.

Despite our flaws—ingratitude for God's blessings, unfaithfulness to God and a love of earthly things, unattractive thoughts and actions—our Bridegroom still loves us. We sin time and time again, proving we are not loyal to Him. But over and over again, Jesus forgives and loves us.

Having made us His Bride, Jesus is preparing a place for us, a new home. One day, He will come again to bring us to be with Him forever. This earth shall pass away, and a new heaven and new earth will be the dwelling place of the Bride (Revelation 21). The Church waits with expectation for that day.

For Christians, the end of the world as we know it doesn't need to fill us with a sense of dread or fear. Instead, we can view the end of this world as the beginning of the next new world. It gives us great hope to know that "the sufferings of this present time are not worth comparing with the glory that is to be revealed to us" (Romans 8:18). At the end of the Bible, Jesus says, "Surely I am coming soon" (Revelation 2:20). Christians agree with the apostle John, who writes, "Amen. Come, Lord Jesus!" (Revelation 22:21). We look forward to the Last Day because it is the time when Jesus will return!

Living the Christian Life

This chapter gives a picture of how the Christian interacts with the world, fellow believers, and God Himself. How do Christians live in the world but not of the world? How do the faithful relate to one another? How do believers live as simultaneously sinners and saints? The Holy Spirit works in us to do the tasks God has prepared for each of us.

God Gives Us Purpose

The Holy Spirit enables us to do things we were never able to do before. We can be kind. We can be loving. We can serve others. And we do these things in joy and freedom, not guilt or obligation. Our salvation is already secure. Now, we share God's love with others through our words and actions.

Review Galatians 5:22–23. This list is called the fruit of the Spirit. How is fruit a great image for these traits?

God Gives Us Freedom

God cleans our hearts of sin and makes us saints and disciples. We have no fear of sin or death; Jesus has conquered it all for us! Made new, we go out into the world in love and service for others.

Review 1 John 4:7–11 to remember the source of the love that we share.

God Gives Us Forgiveness

Forgiveness is essential to the Christian faith. We are all sinners who deserve eternal punishment. But because of our Savior Jesus Christ, our sins are paid for. When we confess our sins, turning away from them, we receive God's forgiveness. God gives us forgiveness through the Means of Grace: the Word and Sacraments (Baptism and Communion). Forgiven by God, we forgive those who sin against us.

Review 1 John 1:8–9 and the importance of confession.

God Gives Us the Church

We are the Body of Christ, many members working together with Christ as the Head. The Church includes all believers, those on earth and those with the Lord. Even if Christians on earth are divided by location or denomination, all believers in Jesus Christ are united as one.

Review Ephesians 4:4–6 to see this emphasis on Christian unity.

God Gives Us Worship

The Lord welcomes us into His house, guarantees His presence, strengthens us with His Word, and feeds us at His Table. Nourished by this Divine Service, we go out into the world to proclaim Christ's love to others.

Review 1 Peter 2:9 to recall our identity and mission in Christ.

God Gives Us a Commission

As we wait for Jesus to return on the Last Day, we serve others, sharing with them the Good News of salvation in Jesus Christ. We pray to God for our needs and for the needs of others.

Review Colossians 3:17 and consider how this perspective affects our actions here on earth.

Living the Christian Life

This page serves two purposes. First, it provides questions for you to consider. But it also provides a blank section to store your own questions.

If you're using this book for personal study, this is a great way to record any questions you still have. Then find a time to meet with a pastor, church leader, or church friend to talk things through. **If you meet with a class**, your questions can help fuel great discussion during class time.

Warning: You might need extra writing space.

God Gives Us Purpose

- How does the Holy Spirit equip you to serve others?

God Gives Us Freedom

- God makes us free to serve in our vocations. What vocations has God given you?

God Gives Us Forgiveness

- Because we are forgiven, we can share that forgiveness with others. Are there people in your life who need your forgiveness?

God Gives Us the Church

- We are all members of the Body of Christ. What skills and talents do you have?

- Think of someone who has a different skill or talent than you have. Thank God for that person, and encourage him or her in that gift.

God Gives Us Worship

- List at least two different blessings we receive in the Divine Service.

- Why is weekly worship such an important part of the Christian life?

God Gives Us a Commission

- We know that Jesus will return soon, so what is our mission as Christians here on earth?

Your Questions

Try a journal or some large adhesive notes.
TIP

CHAPTER 5

Living Forever with Jesus

Basic Bible Teachings

In God's Word, we read that on the Last Day Jesus will raise all the dead. The same bodies that have died and are buried in graves will be made alive, but perfected and whole. Jesus will come down from heaven with a loud command and the trumpet call of God (1 Thessalonians 4:16). Jesus' coming with power and great glory is certainly frightening for those who don't believe in Him. To them, Jesus will bring judgment. But for those who are connected to Him, belonging to the Body of Christ (the Church), we know that this Last Day is really our first day of eternal life with Jesus.

Knowing that Jesus will come again gives us added motivation to spread God's Word to the world so that all may hear of Jesus' love.

Dig a Little Deeper

READ Isaiah 65:17 and 2 Peter 3:13 to hear the promise of new heavens and a new earth.

READ 2 Peter 3:8–15 and consider why the Lord is patient for the Last Day to come.

WHAT DOES THE BIBLE TELL US ABOUT OUR RELATIONSHIP WITH GOD?

Since before time, God loved us and knew us. God created the world just for us. He walked with Adam and Eve in perfect communion. Throughout human history and still today, He desires that we love and trust in Him above all else.

He deserves all honor and praise. There is none like our triune God. It is truly amazing to think that this incomprehensible God would care about us at all. He does. He knows us, every detail of our lives, every sinful detail—and He still loves us and wants to be our God.

God has made it possible for us to be reunited with Him. Through Baptism and the Lord's Supper, through His Word, we experience little glimmers of what perfect communion with God will be like. We wait, with the full confidence of faith and hope, knowing that one day, Jesus will come back and take us to be with Him forever. We will gaze on His beauty and be able to see the fullness of His glory. We will physically walk with God once again, just as He created us to do. This time, it will be forever.

"For this reason I bow my knees before the Father, . . . that you, being rooted and grounded in love, may have strength . . . to know the love of Christ that surpasses knowledge, that you may be filled with all the fullness of God. Now to Him who is able to do far more abundantly than all that we ask or think, according to the power at work within us, to Him be glory . . . throughout all generations, forever and ever. Amen" (Ephesians 3:14, 17–21).

WHAT HAPPENS WHEN WE DIE?

The Bible tells us that when we die, we are immediately with Jesus in God's presence. Until Jesus' return on the Last Day, we are in God's presence with our souls, not our bodies. But that is not the end. On the Last Day, all believers in Christ will be raised with perfect, imperishable bodies to be with Jesus in our eternal home.

In the meantime, we take comfort in the truth that physical death is but a sleep (Revelation 14:13).

From Jesus' words, we learn that we need not fear death. We can die in hope, knowing our Lord will call us back to a new, eternal life with Him.

The word *heaven* is used to describe life lived eternally in the presence of God. The Bible leaves most of the details about heaven hidden from us. What we do know is that after we die, we are in the presence of God spiritually. After the Last Day, our resurrected bodies are reunited with our souls in the same presence of God. Our eternal life with Jesus is no longer damaged by the effects of sin. Those who live in the presence of God will live as God intended humans to live from the very beginning—in complete and perfect fellowship and harmony with Him.

God Gives Us Eternal Life

The fullness of our life in the eternal kingdom will be experienced on the Last Day because both our body and soul will be with Christ forever. Jesus will walk among us again! Everything will be perfect, just as it once was with Adam and Eve in the Garden of Eden. Jesus is preparing a new heaven and a new earth. The first heaven and the first earth will be gone (Revelation 21:1).

"Behold, the dwelling place of God is with man. He will dwell with them, and they will be His people, and God Himself will be with them as their God. He will wipe away every tear from their eyes, and death shall be no more, neither shall there be mourning, nor crying, nor pain anymore, for the former things have passed away" (Revelation 21:3–4).

This is our best understanding of heaven, or eternal life.

WHY DO WE ALSO CALL THE LAST DAY THE JUDGMENT DAY?

In the Apostles' Creed, we confess Jesus, who "sits at the right hand of God, the Father Almighty . . . [and] will come to judge the living and the dead."

Jesus is now exercising His divine power over the whole universe. God placed "all things under His feet and gave Him as head over all things to the church, which is His body, the fullness of Him who fills all in all" (Ephesians 1:22–23). As our King, Jesus rules and protects His Church and governs all the world for the benefit of His Church.

The Bible says that Jesus will judge all people, separating the believers from the unbelievers. The Bible uses harvesting language to describe the day. There is no way to sugarcoat what unbelievers will experience during this **Judgment Day**. They, too, will be resurrected in their bodies, but they will be condemned to an eternity completely separated from God, His goodness, His providence and care. In this world, unbelievers are spiritually separated from God and are called by the Gospel. They still benefit from His care of this world. But having rejected the Gospel—the removal of sin for Jesus' sake—in this life, unbelievers will face judgment for their sins on their own. This eternal place of separation is commonly called **hell**. Hell is an eternal punishment: having our own way forever, separated from God. Hell was not made for people, but when mankind sinned, it became a place also for those who have rejected God and have no desire for His love (Matthew 25:41).

CAN WE BE SURE WE WILL GO TO BE WITH GOD?

Christians do not need to be afraid of the coming judgment. Those who believe in Jesus have already been declared "not guilty" because of Jesus' righteousness. His holiness (perfection) and His suffering and death on the cross in our place has removed God's wrath from those who believe in Him. On Judgment Day, no sin will be found in us. Our heavenly Father will welcome us home as His children because of our salvation through His Son.

summing it up

thinking it through

Living Forever with Jesus

God has always loved us, but our sin separated us from Him. Jesus paid the price for our sin and broke the curse of death so that all who believe in Him will be saved from eternal separation from God. When Jesus returns, all believers will be united with our Lord and with one another in perfect love for all eternity.

God Gives Us Eternal Life

When believers in Jesus Christ die, their spirit, or soul, is with the Lord. When Jesus comes on the Last Day, our resurrected and perfect bodies will be reunited with our souls, and we will live with God forever in the new heavens and new earth.

Review Revelation 21:3–4, and try to imagine a place where there is no suffering or sin.

Living Forever with Jesus

This page serves two purposes. First, it provides questions for you to consider. But it also provides a blank section to store your own questions.

If you're using this book for personal study, this is a great way to record any questions you still have. Then find a time to meet with a pastor, church leader, or church friend to talk things through. **If you meet with a class**, your questions can help fuel great discussion during class time.

Warning: You might need extra writing space.

God Gives Us Eternal Life

- Try to consider forever. When we think of our first years here on earth, how does that change the perspective of our suffering? How does it change the perspective of our mission?

Your Questions

Try a journal or some large adhesive notes. TIP

Absolution: Literally, "set free." This Latin term was used by theologians as a translation of the biblical word *aphiemi*, meaning "to set free, cancel, or forgive."

Angel: A spirit being, created by God, having a mind and will but no physical body (though, at times, for God's purposes, angels have taken on a human form). There are good angels and those that turned evil.

Apostle: One of Jesus' original disciples or Paul, chosen by God to preach the Gospel; one sent directly by Christ into the world to carry out the Great Commission (Matthew 28:18–20).

Atonement: From an old French term for being "at one." Reconciliation between parties that were previously divided. One man's life given as a sacrifice and ransom to redeem all others.

Baptism: From the Greek word meaning "to immerse" or "to wash." Many religions have religious washings. But Christian Baptism applies water "in the name of the Father and of the Son and of the Holy Spirit" as described by Jesus (Matthew 28:19). In Baptism, God washes away the person's sins and welcomes that person as a member of His kingdom. Through water joined to God's Word, the Holy Spirit puts to death our sinful nature, connects us to Christ in His death and resurrection, and gives us new spiritual birth as God's children.

Bible: God's inspired Word; a collection of books by many authors about God and His plan of salvation for humankind.

Bless: (1) To give joy or gifts. (2) To pray for someone's welfare. (3) To give God glory and praise. God blesses us with His good gifts; we bless Him with our thanks and praise.

Blessing: Divine help, favor, protection, encouragement, or approval.

Body of Christ: A term given to all believers; like the human body with its many parts, the Body of Christ has many members. Each believer is a member of Christ's body; believers work together to accomplish the Lord's mission of spreading the Gospel throughout the world.

Born again: Through the Gospel, the Holy Spirit makes us reborn. In Baptism, the Holy Spirit creates faith in a believer; he or she becomes a child of God and begins a new life as a new person, no longer hostile to God. We have a new nature because our sinful nature has been drowned.

Catholic: (Greek *katholikos*: "universal" or "general.") A term first applied to the Christian Church as a whole in a letter of Ignatius (ca. AD 110): "Where Christ is, there is the catholic Church." In Lutheran theology (as in early Christendom), the word is often used of the one holy catholic ("Christian") and apostolic Church united to Christ by faith, and transcending time, space, and all other barriers.

Christ: Greek for "Messiah," which is Hebrew for "Anointed One."

Church: (1) A place where believers meet to worship God. (2) A congregation, or group of people, that meet together regularly for worship. (3) A denomination in the Christian faith; a group of people who agree on certain points of Christianity. (4) All believers, on earth and in heaven, who believe in Jesus Christ as their Lord and Savior.

Communion: (1) To take part in something; to share something. In the Lord's Supper, communicants (people who receive Holy Communion) partake of the body and blood of Christ and are made members of His Body, the Church. "Communion" or "participation" translates the Greek word for fellowship, *koinonia*. (2) Another name for the Sacrament of the Altar.

Condemn: To declare guilty and deserving of hell because of rebellious unbelief.

Confession: (1) Stating accurately what we believe is true. (2) The act by which one admits or confesses sin(s) and the guilt of sin.

Confirmation: Rite designed to help a person identify with the life and mission of the Church.

Congregation: A local gathering of Christians who come together for worship.

Conscience: An inner sense of right and wrong written into our hearts at creation, but unreliable since the fall into sin; needs to be guided by God's Word.

Conversion: A change, turnaround, transformation; new life in Christ.

Covenant: A promise or pledge; a formal agreement. An agreement of faithfulness. "I will walk among you and will be your God, and you shall be My people" (Leviticus 26:12).

Creation: (1) The act of making something out of nothing, of bringing into existence. (2) All that God has created, that is, everything in existence.

Creed: From the Latin word *credo*, "I believe"; a summary of what the Church believes; refers to any of the three Ecumenical Creeds used in worship: the Apostles' Creed, often used at Baptisms, funerals, and non-Communion services; the Nicene Creed, often used at services with Holy Communion; and the Athanasian Creed, often spoken on Trinity Sunday.

Death: (1) End of life. (2) Rending apart of two things that were once closely joined. The fall into sin broke the fellowship between God and humankind. Physical death is the separation of the body and soul (Ecclesiastes 12:7); spiritual death is separation from God in this life (Isaiah 59:2). Eternal death is being separated from God forever, in hell. We will never "cease to exist." Unbelievers will experience a permanent separation from God, but will be in this state for eternity.

Denomination: A religious organization uniting congregations in a single administrative body.

Devil: Another name for Satan; this name means "slanderer" or "accuser." Because of Jesus' death on the cross, our heavenly Father does not listen to Satan's accusations.

Disciple: One who listens, understands, and follows the teachings and beliefs of another.

Doctrine: A belief or set of beliefs that is taught (teaching of the Bible, or a teaching of a denomination).

Eternal: Created beings (humans, angels) with eternal life have a beginning but no end. God is eternal, without beginning or end.

Faith: God's gift of belief in Christ for the forgiveness of sins, life, salvation, and all that we need; trust.

Fall, the: The first sin, committed by Adam and Eve. Humankind fell from its perfect state, ruining God's whole creation. Our sinful nature is a result of the fall.

Father: The First Person of the Trinity; the Creator, who sits on the throne.

Fellowship: Doing something together; joining with other Christians to hear God's Word and receive His Sacrament.

Flesh, the: Sinful human nature.

Forgiveness: Through Christ, our wrongdoings are taken away and forgotten. We forgive others in thanksgiving for God's forgiveness.

Glory: The majesty and power revealed by God; worshipful praise, honor, and thanksgiving to God.

Good works: A response of faith; good works naturally flow from the faith God gives to us.

Gospel: The message of Christ's death and resurrection for the forgiveness of sins, eternal life, and salvation. The Holy Spirit works through the Gospel in Word and Sacrament to create and sustain faith and to empower good works. The Gospel is found in both the Old and New Testaments.

Grace: The unearned and undeserved gift of forgiveness and eternal life received by faith and given to all who believe. Ephesians 2:8–9 shows us that this gift is free to those who receive it but was purchased at great cost by Jesus' life, death on the cross, and resurrection.

Guilt: The fact of having broken a law or commandment of God.

Heaven: The place where believers in Christ will spend eternity in the presence of God Himself.

Hell: Having our own way forever, separated from God.

Holy: Set apart for a sacred purpose; pure, without sin.

Holy Spirit: The Third Person in the Holy Trinity, true God with the Father and the Son. Sent by Jesus after His resurrection to call people by the Gospel, enlighten them with His gifts, and sanctify them (make them holy). Also known as the Comforter.

Image (of God): To be made without sin, perfectly knowing and gladly doing God's will.

Incarnate/incarnation: In the flesh, in human form. Jesus, true God, became true man.

Inspired: Guided directly by a message from God. "Breathed into"; the Holy Spirit inspired men to write God's Word in the Bible.

Intercede/intercession: To act between parties to reconcile differences; to speak or ask for mercy on behalf of another. Jesus intercedes for us to the Father.

Jesus: Greek form of Joshua or Jeshua; "the Lord saves."

Judgment: A divine sentence or decision; God is the supreme judge of all people. Because of sin, all are guilty of God's wrath. Jesus took our punishment upon Himself.

Judgment Day: Also known as the Last Day, the second coming, Christ's return. Jesus will separate believers and unbelievers.

Justification: What God does *for us* through Jesus. We are rescued by Jesus' death and resurrection.

Kingdom (of God): A kingdom is an area or group of people headed by a king; God's kingdom, or the kingdom of heaven, is made up of all believers.

Law: (1) God's will; God's commands of goodness in thought, word, and deed, and expressions of His punishment and condemnation of sin; the Ten Commandments. (2) Statute, rule, command, instruction, decree, ordinance, requirement, regulation, mandate, precept, order, direction, summons, obligation.

Liturgy: The order Christians follow in public worship. Liturgy may be highly formal or more flexible, but it always has some structure that allows worshipers to participate together. A liturgy usually includes hymns, Confession and Absolution, a creed, Bible readings, a sermon, prayers, the Lord's Prayer, Holy Communion, and a benediction.

Lutheran: A Protestant denomination that shares Martin Luther's understanding of the Bible's main teachings.

Means of Grace: The means by which God gives us the forgiveness, life, and salvation won by the death and resurrection of Christ: God's Word, Absolution, Baptism, and the Lord's Supper.

Merciful: Characterized by compassion, pity, concern; the willingness to help someone in need, especially an enemy.

Mercy: Not receiving punishment you deserve; the kindness and grace of God that does not hold our sins against us, but freely forgives us for Christ's sake.

Messiah: Hebrew for "Anointed One."

Mission: Task; goal; assignment. It is a calling by God to go out and proclaim His Word to the nations. Jesus gave us the Great Commission in Matthew 28:18–20. Missionaries are people who are sent.

Office of the Keys: The authority given to the Church of God to forgive the sins of repentant sinners and to bind sins to unrepentant sinners.

Omniscient: An attribute of God; His perfect knowledge of all things.

Original sin: Sin into which we are born, inherited from Adam and Eve.

Parable: Story using common things to teach spiritual truths.

Pastor: Latin for "shepherd"; the title for the congregation's public minister who is ordained and called to be the spiritual supervisor of the "flock" (congregation) that gathers around Word and Sacrament to receive God's gifts.

Praise: To offer thanks and honor to God; to glorify Him; often done in hymns and songs.

Prayer: Calling upon God, asking for His help and blessing, offering praise and thanksgiving, and bringing our requests before Him.

Prophet: One who speaks a message from God (can be a prediction or warning or an encouragement).

Providence: Divine activity of God in which He uninterruptedly upholds (preserves), governs, and directs lifeless creation, plant life, animal life, humankind and all that concerns humankind, heaven, hell, and everything.

Real presence: In the Sacrament of the Altar, the body and blood of Jesus are actually present with the bread and wine. By the power of His Word, Jesus gives His body and blood in, with, and under the consecrated (blessed) bread and wine.

Reconciliation: The act of repairing a broken relationship, forgiving one another and bringing peace. God does this for us through Jesus.

Redeem: To buy back or to pay a debt owed by someone else. Jesus came to redeem all people from slavery to sin and death. He paid the price to set us free not with money but with His own blood.

Repentance: The turning away from sin toward faith in Christ and His sacrifice for us; a change of heart and renewed trust for God that leads to changed behaviors.

Resurrection: Act of coming back to life after having been dead.

Reveal: To uncover. God is known (uncovered) through Word and Sacrament. Jesus Christ is the Word Incarnate (in the flesh); through Him we see God.

Righteousness: Holiness; freedom from guilt and sin; purity of heart and goodness of life.

Sacrament: From the Greek word meaning "mystery"; literally, "something sacred." In the Lutheran Church, a Sacrament is a sacred act that (1) was instituted by God, (2) has a visible element, and (3) offers the forgiveness of sins earned by Christ. The Sacraments include Baptism, the Lord's Supper, and also Absolution (if one counts the pastor as the visible element; Large Catechism IV 74; Apology XIII 4–5).

Sacred: Honored as holy and dedicated to God.

Saint: The word *saint* in Scripture refers to believers on earth (Acts 9:32; Romans 1:7) and in heaven (Matthew 27:52). Throughout Church history, it has been used to designate one set apart as especially holy (e.g., St. Paul, St. Francis of Assisi). The Lutheran Reformation rejected prayers and devotions to saints. In Lutheran usage, the title of "saint" is not used for anyone except those who were called such before the Reformation.

Salvation: God's action in rescuing or saving us from sin, death, and the devil for Christ's sake.

Sanctification: To make separate; to make holy. The spiritual growth that follows justification by grace through faith in Christ. Sanctification is God's work through His Means of Grace: Word and Sacrament. It is what God does *in us* through the Holy Spirit. We are set free by the empowering gifts of the Spirit. The ongoing work of the Holy Spirit to keep us in the faith, strengthen that faith, and live a life of faith.

Sanctuary: (1) A consecrated place of safety, peace, and meditation. (2) A place set aside where we worship God—God's house.

Satan: The chief of the fallen angels; created holy by God, Satan later rebelled against Him. The name *Satan* means "adversary." He is the enemy of God and God's people.

Savior: Jesus Christ, the one who saves people from their sins.

Scripture: God's Word; in Jesus' time, this would have been what we call the Old Testament today.

Sin: Betraying God; rejecting His will and His ways; any thought, word, or deed that departs from the will of God.

Sinful nature: Our human nature, after the fall, is thoroughly corrupted by sin, making us God's enemies and lovers of ourselves.

Son: The Second Person of the Trinity, our Savior Jesus Christ.

Soul: The breath of life from God that gives the rational immortal spirit by which humans are distinguished from animals.

Sponsor: One who assumes responsibility for a person or cause (e.g., the spiritual nurture of a baptized child).

Temptation: Act or suggestion that leads to the committing of sin.

Testament: A will that established the disposition of one's belongings at the time of death, or a covenant established by God between God and man. The Lord's Supper fulfills both definitions: prior to the cross, Jesus leaves Christians His body and blood for the forgiveness of their sins, and this Sacrament is part of His covenant of grace for man.

Thanksgiving: Offering thanks for the good things we have received.

Triune: The one true God in three persons: Father, Son, and Holy Spirit; Three in One; Trinity.

Vocation: The work in which a person is engaged. Our roles are callings from God. The day-to-day tasks that all of these entail are holy before God. Through our vocations, we love and serve the different neighbors whom God brings to us.

Word: The expression of the will of God; the Holy Scriptures; Jesus—the Word made flesh.

Worship: The service to which God calls and gathers His people to give to them the gifts of life and salvation by means of Word and Sacrament.

WHO WAS MARTIN LUTHER?

The fifteenth-century world into which Martin Luther was born differed greatly from the world of today. Everyone in his European hometown of Eisleben, Germany, held the same worldview. They were told what to believe by the priests of the Medieval Church. Few could read, and even if they could read, Bibles were scarce and written in Latin, a language known only by those with much education.

By and large, the people were fearful and superstitious. They believed that forces of evil could be kept away through pious actions, such as visiting holy places and repeating holy words without even giving thought to their meaning. The Medieval Church had fallen way from the teachings of God's Word, which explain salvation, forgiveness of sins, and the power for a new life as gifts of God. These gifts were earned by Jesus through His innocent life and His death on the cross to pay for the sins of all people.

Like others alive at this time, Luther's hardworking and strict parents taught their children to serve and obey God so that they might go to heaven when they died. People were afraid of God and His punishment for their sins; they thought they had to do good works to gain God's favor.

Once, when caught in a violent thunderstorm, young Luther prayed that if he survived the storm, he would become a monk and live a life of poverty and obedience in service to God. As a monk and a worker in the Church, Luther continued his education in theology. As he studied, he was able to read the Bible on His own. From God's Word, Luther learned God was a loving God who had created him and given him freely the gifts of forgiveness and salvation.

WHAT DID MARTIN LUTHER DO?

Though his father wanted him to become a lawyer, Martin Luther felt called to serve the Church. He did serve, first as a monk, then as a priest and theology professor at a university. Through his study of God's Word, Luther came to recognize that God loves people and that He gives forgiveness and salvation as a free gift to all who believe in Jesus. The gifts Jesus provides for free we could not earn even if we tried.

MARTIN LUTHER

The Church in Luther's day taught something very different. Although the Church taught that Jesus died for the sins of the world, it also taught that people could buy forgiveness through indulgences, even before committing sins. Indulgences were official pieces of paper guaranteeing forgiveness, issued with the support and backing of the pope himself. Luther became concerned that many who purchased indulgences showed no sorrow over their sins. In addition, Luther could find nothing in God's Word promoting indulgences and other Church practices, such as praying to Mary and the saints.

Luther argued against those teachings and practices of the Church that had no basis in God's Word. On October 31, 1517, Luther posted Ninety-Five Theses (statements for discussion and debate, questioning some of the Church's current practices and teachings), knowing that many people would be attending mass for All Saints' Day and would see it. His ideas spread quickly because the recently invented printing press made widespread distribution of his books possible.

Eventually, Luther was accused of heresy (false teaching) and was excommunicated. He was called to a trial before the political leader of the day, Emperor Charles V. When Luther was asked to take back (recant) his statements against the Church, Luther replied, "Unless I am convinced by Scripture and plain reason, I do not accept the authority of popes and councils, for they have contradicted each other. My conscience is captive to the Word of God. I cannot and I will not recant anything, for to go against my conscience is neither right nor safe. Here I stand. God help me. Amen." While in hiding, Luther translated the Bible into German so that ordinary people could read God's Word for themselves, in their own language.

Luther boldly stood up for what he knew to be right against a crowd of powerful rulers who accused and threatened him. He trusted in God's truth and power to give him strength.

WHAT IS THE LUTHERAN CHURCH?

The Lutheran Church follows the teachings of Martin Luther, but Luther would be the first to say that his teachings were not his own. His teachings and thoughts were based on Scripture: the very words of God Himself. Luther's teachings were not new; he proclaimed that the Church should uphold the old teachings of the prophets and apostles and stay true to Scripture alone, not adding to it and not reinventing it.

For Martin Luther, the problem was not mainly the morality of the clergy, or even its ineptitude, but how the Church thought and taught about salvation. Luther saw that at the very center there was deformation and error in the Church of his time. This error had consequences not only for the understanding of how people are saved but also in the area of how the Sacraments are understood, what the Church is, what the Church's ministry is, and what the Christian life looks like. The Lutheran Reformation attempted to change only what was necessary and did not try to start a new Church and discard fifteen hundred years of Church history.

Lutherans believe the following:

- The faith and preaching of the Church is centered in Christ crucified. The heart of our faith is that Jesus Christ is Lord.
- We worship the triune God: three persons in one God (God the Father, God the Son, and God the Holy Spirit).

- We confess the three creeds of the Christian Church: the Apostles', Nicene, and Athanasian.
- We emphasize Sola Scriptura (Scripture alone), Sola Gratia (Grace alone), and Sola Fide (Faith alone).
- The Lutheran Church accepts without reservation all the documents contained in the Book of Concord of 1580 as a true and unadulterated statement and exposition of the Word of God. It contains these documents:
    - The Augsburg Confession, a statement of faith written by Philip Melanchthon and read before emperor Charles V at Augsburg, Germany, in 1530. While friendly in tone, it was adopted as a testimony against abuses prevalent in the Church and against the errors of certain reformers regarding such crucial doctrines as original sin and the sacraments.
    - The Apology (Defense) of the Augsburg Confession, also written by Melanchthon. It, too, became an official confession of faith among Lutherans by its adoption at Smalcald, Germany, in 1527. In great detail, it answers criticism of the Augsburg Confession. Virtually half of the Apology of the Augsburg Confession is

devoted to the biblical doctrine of justification by grace through faith in Jesus Christ.

- The Smalcald Articles, written by Luther in 1536 and signed by many clergy present at Smalcald in 1537. The Articles are a summary of Luther's main disagreements with the Roman Church. Melanchthon's Treatise on the Power and Primacy of the Pope was also officially adopted at Smalcald.
- The Formula of Concord, completed in 1577. Served to resolve doctrinal differences among Lutherans and was approved by over eight thousand theologians, pastors, and teachers by 1580. It was not a new confession, but an exposition and defense of the previously adopted writings.
- The Small Catechism, the best known and most widely used of the Book of Concord documents. It was completed in 1529 by Luther and was originally intended to be a helpful manual for pastors and family heads in teaching God's Word to children and adults.
- The Large Catechism, also completed in 1529 by Luther. It is not made up of questions and answers but presents basic Christian teachings in a form often used in sermons.

We have open arms to receive God's grace and to embrace the world with God's love. Lutherans are "evangelical" because they proclaim the Gospel (Good News), which is what the word originally meant. But Lutherans are not a part of the Evangelical movement begun in Great Britain in 1730 that emphasizes personal conversion and being born again. The Good News is that Jesus has done it all for us, procuring our salvation (which includes calling us to faith).

LUTHERAN LITURGY

Lutherans follow an order of worship based exclusively on Scripture and focused completely on Jesus. Through the Word and Sacraments, God speaks to His people.

The order of service is not unique to Lutherans. It is the ancient form of worship that has been developed among Christians all over the world, from the start of Christianity.

THE PREPARATION

The Invocation: From the Latin for "call upon"; the words "In the name of the Father and of the Son and of the Holy Spirit" spoken at the beginning of the service; serves as a reminder of Holy Baptism.

Confession and Absolution: Confession is the act by which one admits or confesses sin(s) and the guilt of sin. The expression "We are by nature sinful and unclean" comes from the Augsburg Confession (XI 1). The statements made in this prayer of confession are a summary of Romans 7:14–8:14. *Absolution* literally means "set free." This Latin term was used as a translation of the biblical word *aphiemi*, meaning "to set free, cancel, or forgive."

THE SERVICE OF THE WORD

Introit: A collection of passages from Scripture that set the tone for the service; verses are different each Sunday.

The Kyrie: *Kyrie eleison*. Greek for "Lord, have mercy." The Kyrie is the first prayer of the congregation in the Divine Service; it is a cry for mercy that our Lord and King will hear us and help us in our needs and troubles. It is a litany.

The Hymn of Praise or Gloria in Excelsis: Confident that the Lord is merciful and has forgiven us, we join the whole Church and all the angels in singing glory to God.

The Salutation and Collect: The Salutation shows the special relationship between the congregation and the pastor, God's representative. It is a greeting found often in the Bible. The Collect is the pastor's first prayer in the name of the people, as he speaks for the congregation. It "collects" the theme for the day in a concise way. Most of the Collects have been used in the Church for over fifteen hundred years.

The Readings from Scripture: Selected portions of God's Word are appointed to be read according to the arrangement of the Church Year. Traditionally, the congregation is seated for the Old Testament Readings and Epistle, since these are instructional. The congregation stands for the reading of the Gospel, which is an account of the life and words of Jesus.

The Creed: A solemn confession and response of faith to the Word.

The Hymn of the Day: Chief hymn of the Divine Service; a hymn specifically selected to reflect the theme of the day, especially the Holy Gospel.

The Sermon: The preacher explains God's Word.

The Offering: Symbolizes the "spiritual worship" (Romans 12:1) of Christian lives offered in response to God and unites the faithful in an act of fellowship (Acts 2:42).

The Prayer of the Church: Prayers that what has been heard may be taken to heart and that God would take care of our needs. We give God thanks, praise, and honor.

The Offertory: Praises God for His many benefits to our lives. Used to accompany our gifts (offerings) as they are given to the Lord.

THE SERVICE OF THE SACRAMENT

The Preface: Proclamation of praise and thanksgiving that begins the Service of the Sacrament. A dialogue between pastor and the people used since the Early Church.

Proper Preface: A special prayer said before the Lord's Supper that emphasizes the key themes of the feast, occasion, or season of the Church Year.

The Sanctus: Latin for "holy"; follows the Preface in the Service of the Sacrament; based on Isaiah 6:3 and Matthew 21:9.

Hosanna: Means "Lord, save us." An expression of joy for what Christ has done.

Benedictus: Latin for the first words, "Blessed is he." We join with all the company of heaven in singing these words from Psalm 118:26.

Prayer of Thanksgiving: Offered at the altar by the pastor on behalf of the congregation. Thanks God for instituting the Sacrament for our forgiveness.

The Lord's Prayer: The model prayer Jesus taught to the disciples (Matthew 6:9–13). Sometimes it is called the Our Father, after the first words of the prayer.

The Words of Institution: The words spoken by Christ when He instituted the Sacrament of the Altar (Matthew 26:26–28; Mark 14:22–24; Luke 22:19–20; 1 Corinthians 11:23–25); the pastor speaks these very words of Christ in the Service of the Sacrament at the consecration of the bread and wine.

The Pax Domini: In anticipation of the blessings to be received, the pastor and people announce the peace of God to one another (John 20:19).

The Agnus Dei: Latin for "Lamb of God" (John 1:29); we adore the Savior who is present in the Holy Meal.

The Distribution: We receive the body and blood of Jesus Christ for the forgiveness of sins.

The Post-Communion Canticle: A hymn of thanks. Usually the Nunc Dimittis ("Depart in peace"), also called "Simeon's Song" (Luke 2:29–32).

The Prayer of Thanksgiving: Prayer that the gifts now received from the Lord may accomplish His purpose in His people.

The Benediction: From the Latin for "[The Lord] bless [you]"; the Aaronic Blessing (Numbers 6:24–26) is commonly used in connection with Holy Communion, while the Apostolic Blessing (2 Corinthians 13:14) is used at other times.

People often think that worship is about what we do for or toward God. The reality is quite different. In the Divine Service, God comes to us and provides His service for us. The work we do in worship is to receive the gift of God's grace and respond.

CHURCH YEAR CALENDAR

The Christian Church Year is used not only to mark time but also to set the story of Jesus in an orderly pattern for teaching.

The Church Year is divided into three parts: the Time of Christmas, the Time of Easter, and the Time of the Church. The Time of Christmas deals with who Jesus is: God in the flesh. The Time of Easter deals with what Jesus came to do: save us through His death and resurrection. The Time of the Church deals with how the Lord of the Church, Jesus, is at work in the members of the Body of Christ.

Advent: Advent starts four Sundays before Christmas and ends on December 24.

Color: The color for the season of Advent is blue to emphasize hope and preparation for Jesus' coming. You may also see violet used during Advent as a symbol of repentance to remind us to feel sorry for our sins.

Christmas: About three hundred years after Jesus was born, Christians chose December 25 as the day we celebrate the nativity, or birth, of Jesus. The Christmas season begins on Christmas Eve and ends on January 5. This season is also known as the twelve days of Christmas.

Color: The color for the season of Christmas is white.

Epiphany: Epiphany is on January 6. The season continues until the day before Ash Wednesday. *Epiphany* means "to show" or "to make known." It is often called the Gentile Christmas because it is the celebration of when the Magi, who were Gentiles, came to worship Jesus.

Color: The color for most of the season of Epiphany is green. White is used on the Day of Epiphany, the Baptism of Our Lord, and the Transfiguration.

Lent: The season begins on Ash Wednesday, when we remember that "the wages of sin is death" and that our bodies came from ashes/dust and will become ashes/dust again after we die. The season is forty days long (not counting the Sundays in Lent). During Lent, we focus on our need to repent of our sins and our need of a Savior from sin.

Color: The color for the season is violet, although the color for Ash Wednesday and Good Friday is black. The color for Maundy Thursday is white. Many churches take everything off the altar and drape it with black cloth on Good Friday.

Holy Week: The final week of Lent. Includes Palm Sunday, Maundy (Holy) Thursday, Good Friday, and Easter Vigil.

Easter Day and Post-Easter Season: Easter Sunday is celebrated on the first Sunday after the first full moon falling on or after March 21 (the first day of spring). The season of Easter is fifty days.

Color: The color for Easter and its season is white.

Pentecost: Pentecost is celebrated fifty days after Easter. It celebrates the fulfillment of Jesus' promise to send the Holy Spirit to the Church.

Color: Red, the color of fire and blood, is the color for Pentecost.

Post-Pentecost Season: The Sundays after Pentecost make up the longest portion of the Church Year. We focus on growing together in the life God has given us through the Means of Grace.

Color: The color for most of the season is green.

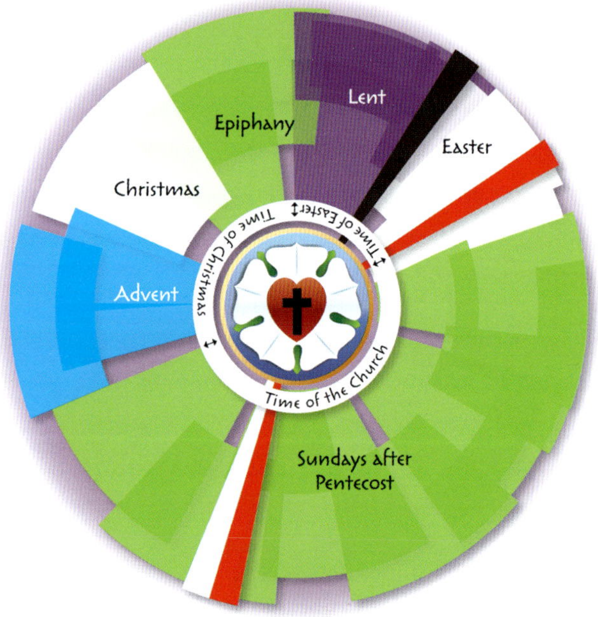